# THE
# BAPTIZED
# LIFE

# THE BAPTIZED LIFE

## The Lifelong Meaning of Immersion into Christ

## TOM A. JONES

**DPI**

DISCIPLESHIP
PUBLICATIONS
INTERNATIONAL

dpibooks.org

**The Baptized Life**

©2013 by DPI Books
5016 Spedale Court #331
Spring Hill, TN 37174

Printed in the United States of America

Cover Design: Brian Branch
Interior Design: Thais Gloor
978-1-57782-246-9

# Contents

# INTRODUCTION

*Scene One:* An outdoor location near London with a makeshift pool, seemingly the focal point of a crowd. Eighty-year-old Alex gives greetings to the group of well-wishers who surround him. A widower since losing his wife to Alzheimer's disease four years earlier, he has been living with his daughter and son-in-law. In their home he has seen a constant flow of people coming for Bible studies and discussions. He has witnessed the closeness of Christian relationships.

Most importantly, he has seen the peace that comes from trusting God and seeking first his Kingdom. He understands it is never too late to surrender to God's purposes, and after he confesses that Jesus is Lord, two men carefully lower him into the pool, immersing him completely. Then they lift him out of the water as he flashes a radiant smile.

***Scene Two:*** A rugged area of Colorado by a rushing mountain stream. Tyler stands on the bank as a crowd of friends share about his openness and his heart to obey God. He then describes his journey through atheism, his fascination with science, but finally how a scene from the movie *Les Miserables* brought a complete change of perspective and opened him up to the truth of the gospel.

He states his faith in the death, burial and resurrection of Jesus, confesses that "Jesus is Lord" and then steps into the icy and powerful water. Two friends immerse him in the name of the Father, the Son and the Holy Spirit. Others throw towels around the trio as they emerge joyfully from the water. An engineer now has something new to build.

***Scene Three:*** An apartment in a city in China. Jia Li (not her real name) is there to do something she could not have imagined three years earlier. Before she met Mei-Lien (not her real name) on her university campus, she had considered herself an atheist. It took some time, but she came to consider her new friend an angel sent from the God she was starting to believe in.

However, that didn't mean she was ready for a commitment to Jesus. Some of the women studied the Bible with her for two years, but it was only after she went through some particularly difficult challenges that her heart was softened.

Now she is here, in her words, "to please God and let him—and not people—be the only Lord in my life." There before a small group of disciples she confesses Jesus, steps into an improvised baptistery and is united with him in his death, burial and resurrection.

***Scene Four:*** Beirut, Lebanon, in the tumultuous Middle East. In a strange sight reminiscent of an incident in the Gospels, several men struggle to carry Samir. They are using a sheet to take him to a handmade tub constructed by his twin brother and now filled with water.

Months earlier, Samir had been in the prime of life when everything was changed by a tragic accident that left him paralyzed from the neck down. Even with multiple surgeries, doctors had doubted he would even talk again. However, he not only spoke, but stayed open to the good news of the Kingdom.

Now he confesses Jesus to be Lord just before his friends lower him into the tub and immerse him in the name of the Father, Son and Spirit. Months earlier all meaning had seemed to end for Samir. Now he is being raised to a new life and a new hope.

During forty-six years of seeking to be a disciple of Jesus, I have seen hundreds of men and women baptized in various settings from warm lakes in summer to a pond where we had to break the November ice, from well-equipped baptisteries with nice dressing rooms to Rubbermaid water troughs used for a purpose never envisioned by the manufacturer.

I have been there at various times of the day and night, as men and women had the kind of experience shared by Alex, Tyler, Jia Li and Samir. While not all of these times were equally dramatic, every story was unique and precious to God. Every such moment was a time of celebration filled with singing and hugs. Every life given over to God was changed. Everyone who was buried with Christ rose to a new life.

About nine months prior to the publication of this book, a young single professional woman, who herself had confessed Jesus as Lord and had been baptized into Christ only a couple of years earlier, came to me seeking a recommendation of a book on baptism. When I later heard from her that the books I recommended had not been that helpful, the seeds and motivation were planted for this volume.

Driven to write a book on biblical baptism that would be practical and encouraging, yet one that would represent a fresh look at the subject, I thought of a statement I read four years ago:

> There is no story but God's; no God but the Father,
> Son and Spirit; and no life but the baptized life.[1]

Those words are from *The Divine Embrace: Recovering the Passionate Spiritual Life* by Professor Robert Webber, the renowned, but sometimes controversial, Baptist theologian who died in 2007. I remember reading that statement and thinking that, while I had read many works devoted to baptism, I had never heard that phrase—"the baptized life." But it rang true. It resonated. And so we will examine the baptized life.

---

1. Robert Webber, *The Divine Embrace: Recovering the Passionate Spiritual Life* (Grand Rapids: Baker Books, 2006), 27.

# FROM HEAVEN OR FROM MEN?

Robert Webber sees baptism as a crucial New Testament theme and a key to a passionate spiritual life, and he makes this poignant comment:

> Baptism, while it may occur in a moment of time, is a state of continual being. We are called to live daily in our baptism. Those who do not live in the divine embrace where their new identity has been established in baptism should not make a claim to have it. Baptism is a way of life.[1]

Baptism as a way of life. This idea reminds me of an often overlooked statement by Martin Luther, one of the great Protestant reformers:

> For this reason let everyone esteem his Baptism as a daily dress in which he is to walk constantly, that he

---

1. Webber, *The Divine Embrace,* 153.

may ever be found in the faith and its fruits, that he suppress the old man and grow up in the new.[2]

Another vivid image—baptism as a daily dress, a statement reminiscent of Galatians 3:26–27. With this, Luther is also saying that Christians should stay in the spirit of their baptism throughout their lives.

But long before Webber and Luther there was this statement:

> But we, little fishes after the example of our Ichthus (ΙΧΘΥΣ), Jesus Christ, are born in water, nor have we safety in any other way than by permanently abiding in water.[3]

So wrote the early church father, Tertullian (d.220 AD), who was saying Christians find spiritual safety by abiding in the same water they were born in—that is their baptism.

But ultimately, all of these statements—modern and ancient—find their inspiration in Paul's words to the Romans in chapter 6, and I place them here from the Phillips Translation:

> Now what is our response to be? Shall we sin to our heart's content and see how far we can exploit the grace of God? What a ghastly thought! We, who have died to sin—how could we live in sin a moment longer? Have you forgotten that all of us who were

2. Martin Luther, *The Larger Catechism*, XIII A.
3. Tertulian, *On Baptism*, Chapter 1.

baptised [sic] into Jesus Christ were, by that very action, sharing in his death? We were dead and buried with him in baptism, so that just as he was raised from the dead by that splendid Revelation of the Father's power so we too might rise to life on a new plane altogether. (vv1–5)

In so many words Paul is the one saying, "Shall we go on sinning so that grace may increase? No way! A ghastly thought! Don't you remember your baptism—how you died with Christ and were buried with Christ and rose up to a whole new life? Now live your baptism. Live that baptized life!"

So we see this idea of living the baptized life has a rich history because it captured a profound New Testament idea.

### *The Power of Baptism*

In an environment where discussions about baptism are often, sadly, quite contentious, the main purpose of this book is not to deal with some of the disputable questions about the proper mode of Christian baptism or what formula should be recited when baptism is carried out, or even what age person is a candidate for baptism or how much one needs to understand when being baptized. The main purpose is not to give a lawyerly mound of evidence to prove that one group's theology and practice of baptism is the correct one and that others are wrong.

The main purpose of this work, instead, is to shine a light on the spiritual richness and power of baptism. It is a vital biblical practice mentioned dozens of times in the New Testament, showing that for every disciple of Jesus, baptism must be a treasured past event kept vividly alive in our minds and hearts so that it has dramatic continuing consequences. In doing so, we will address any issue we find that relates to the biblical material, and hopefully, we will all allow the Scriptures to bring correction wherever it is needed.

At one point in his ministry Jesus was in a discussion with the Pharisees, and Matthew tells us:

> Jesus replied, "I will also ask you one question. If you answer me, I will tell you by what authority I am doing these things. John's baptism—where did it come from? Was it from heaven, or from men?"
>
> They discussed it among themselves and said, "If we say, 'From heaven,' he will ask, 'Then why didn't you believe him?' But if we say, 'From men'—we are afraid of the people, for they all hold that John was a prophet."
>
> So they answered Jesus, "We don't know."
>
> Then he said, "Neither will I tell you by what authority I am doing these things." (Matthew 21:24–27)

We could ask the same question about Christian baptism. Was it from heaven, or from men? Certainly most

Christian groups would say it was from heaven and not from men, since with only a few exceptions, groups that claim to be Christian have some place for baptism in their teaching. But, let's think carefully about that: If it was important enough for God to give it, for Jesus to include it in his Great Commission, for it to be preached on the Day of Pentecost, for three thousand people to experience it on that first day when the Spirit was poured out, and for Paul to remind five different churches what a defining moment it was in their lives, doesn't it stand to reason that God had something quite significant in mind when he gave it "from heaven"?

And doesn't it seem odd or, really, quite sad, that in many people's spiritual experience it is at best a marginal idea?

As we transition from the old covenant to the new, we move from a religious system that involved dozens of sacrifices, festivals, feasts, rituals, ceremonial washings and their attendant rules, to a whole new approach where the only matters even remotely of this nature are baptism and the Lord's Supper.

Now living under this new covenant, which is written on human hearts and not on tablets of stone, shouldn't we seek to understand God's purpose for these two practices? Paul tells the Corinthian Christians that they "are weak and sick, and a number…have fallen asleep" because of their mishandling of the Lord's Supper (1 Corinthians 11:30). If that is true of the Lord's Supper, would there be any less concern about baptism? Doesn't this say to us that these are deeply important issues?

### Eyes Fixed on Jesus

Indeed, as we will see, baptism is significant, but here is what we must stress: *Baptism has meaning only as it is related to Jesus Christ.* Because this is such a fundamental fact, our goal throughout this study must be to keep our eyes fixed on Jesus. It is only appropriate to speak of the baptized life if we are talking about something intimately tied to Jesus and a Jesus-centered life.

We will look at baptism because it is found throughout the New Testament in most crucial places. We will see it is no peripheral topic in Scripture. However, as the moon shines persistently in the night sky only because it reflects the sun, so we will see that baptism shines persistently only to the extent that it is related to Jesus, connected to and reflecting his life and transforming power. On its own, like the moon, it is a cold and empty thing, but in a Jesus context, it shines, reminds, even reveals and points us in a needed direction. There is a reason it was given to us by God.

We hope to avoid two equally serious mistakes as we examine this theme. First is the tendency of many evangelicals to minimize baptism. In a way reminiscent of the ancient Greeks, particularly the Gnostics, they want to create a sharp (and unbiblical) divide between what the body does and what the spirit does—between baptism and faith—and then value only that which involves the spirit. We will return to that problem later.

Second is the reaction of others who swing to an equally dangerous extreme, making their view of baptism the ultimate test of Christian genuineness. Seeing the neglect of biblical baptism, they begin to give it too much importance or at least act as if it has some inherent power. When that happens they drift into sacramentalism, ritualism or legalism.

We would all do well to consider Jesus' words found in John 5:39–40:

> "You diligently study the Scriptures because you think that by them you possess eternal life. These are the Scriptures that testify about me, yet you refuse to come to me to have life."

Baptism is a major topic in Scripture, but its meaning will be found in how it testifies about Jesus. We must give biblical emphasis to baptism without ever losing sight of what gives it meaning. Jesus without baptism is an incomplete message. Baptism without Jesus is an absolutely useless religious act. Baptism out of faith in Jesus, to Jesus, into Jesus, to surrender to Jesus and for Jesus is a hinge in every disciple's personal history.

Before we move into the Scriptures, I want to say more about our main theme and then look at the direction our study will take.

### Main Theme

Most of us have not thought of the life of a follower of Jesus as "the baptized life." This is new terminology for us. Based on comments already made, we can see that may be because of a tradition that put overwhelming emphasis on salvation by faith, with baptism being a minor matter. If this describes you, to speak of "the baptized life" would almost distort the gospel and smack of a tendency toward human works.

On the other hand, baptism may have been viewed as a major factor in conversion—that is, in becoming a Christian. However, beyond that, baptism may have seemed to have little to do with the ongoing life of a Christian, except that it is a subject to be explained to potential converts.

In both cases, describing the new life in Jesus Christ as "the baptized life" may not seem quite right. In speaking like this, however, we are reviving a very old idea, as we have already noted. Our baptism is something we are to keep living out as long as we live.

I can still remember my beginning Greek teacher describing the best way to think about the meaning of the perfect tense where a past action with continuing effects is being described. If the word, for example, is "overcome," she would tell us, "Think: I am standing in the state of having overcome." If the example was forgiveness, she would tell us, "Think: I am standing in the state of having been forgiven." The message of this book is quite simply to have us all understand, "I am standing in the state of having been baptized into Jesus, and thus must live like it."

### The Kingdom Life

Finally, let me comment on the approach I will take in our study. Several years ago my friend, fellow teacher and fellow author, Steve Brown, and I taught a series on "Baptism in the New Testament." Steve made a suggestion as we discussed our approach, and it was one I was hesitant about at first, but eventually found most fulfilling.

His idea was for us to go through the New Testament book by book, asking what we can learn about baptism just from reading our English Bibles and trying all the time to draw from the texts as if we had never read the New Testament, but were hearing it for the first time. Instead of being in a "prove it" or "teach it" mode, we sought to be in "discover" mode.

Though it was hard for us not to "stray off" into the meaning of Greek words or a discussion of certain practices and convictions in the second and third century church, or to explain something from John's Gospel based on our own understanding of something we would later encounter in Acts or Paul's letters, we did quite well with our commitment. I had been over these baptismal texts dozens of times in my forty-plus years of teaching, but I saw things I had never seen before.

At the end of our study we listed twenty-five conclusions we could describe with confidence from the scriptures we had read. I was surprised by a few things we could not say. Though I was tempted to begin this book with the details of that study, I decided against it because of the concern that I could lose some readers quickly due to the more technical and repetitious nature of that approach. However, you will see some of the results of that study making its way into this discussion, and an appendix will give you the summary of that material.

There are some fine books in print on the subject of baptism, such as Jack Cottrell's *Baptism: A Biblical Study,* and outstanding scholarly works such as G.R. Beasley-Murray's *Baptism in the New Testament,* that take readers through every text on baptism, and you would gain much from these works.

My plan, however, will be to put the emphasis on the transformational nature of the Kingdom of God that broke into this world in Jesus, and in that context, to see how baptism was related to the entrance into that Kingdom and, even more, to the continual living out of the kingdom life. If, at times, it seems I have wandered from our topic into some other areas that are not related to baptism, understand that baptism, because it is baptism into Jesus and the kingdom life, is related in some sense to everything about living in union with him.

This very fact, I have found, made this a difficult book to write. While working on one chapter, I would feel the need to somehow superimpose several others on it because many ideas are so closely related, but hopefully by the time you have read them all you will have a sense of how so many important biblical concepts converge in baptism.

In his book *New Seeds of Contemplation*, Thomas Merton well describes the goal of the one who seeks God:

> Ultimately the secret of all this is perfect abandonment to the will of God in things you cannot control, and perfect obedience to Him in everything that depends on your own volition, so that in all things, in your interior life and in your outward works for God, you desire only one thing, which is the fulfillment of His will.[4]

4. Thomas Merton, *New Seeds of Contemplation* (New Direction Books: New York City, 1962, reissued 2007), Kindle Version, 196.

As we will see, baptism is something outward, an event in our history, with a deep interior meaning. Our desire is to let it be what God wants it to be, a fulfillment of his will—certainly not one thing more! But, at the same time, not one thing less. As Jesus taught us, we pray, *"Father, your kingdom come, your will be done, on earth as it is in heaven."*

In developing a plan for this book, I once again found inspiration from a statement by Martin Luther. Though he endorsed the practice of infant baptism in a way I cannot support, he still saw the connection the New Testament made between baptism and many other elements of the Christian life.

> In Baptism every Christian has enough to study and to practice all his life. He always has enough to do to believe firmly what Baptism promises and brings— victory over death and the devil, forgiveness of sin, God's grace, the entire Christ, and the Holy Spirit with his gifts. In short the blessings of Baptism are so boundless that if timid nature considers them, it may well doubt whether they could all be true.[5]

With this idea that baptism speaks to us of so many elements in the disciple's life, we will examine connections between baptism and vital subjects. We will see how understanding these and staying "in" them is connected to

---

5. Martin Luther, *The Larger Catechism*, "Holy Baptism," 41.

our relationship to Jesus that brings about a transformed and transforming life.

We will examine what the Scriptures say about baptism and its unity with grace, the Kingdom of God, salvation, the death and resurrection of Jesus, the Holy Spirit, the Body of Christ and faith.

Keep in mind a fundamental premise of this book: The New Testament teaches that our baptism can grow more powerful over time because it is designed to again and again bring us back to Jesus from whom we have so much more to learn.

## Questions for Study and Discussion

1. What understanding of baptism did you have from your early religious training?

2. In that understanding, how was baptism connected with Jesus?

3. What does it mean to you when we say baptism occurs in transformational contexts in the New Testament? How does that relate to your own previous understanding of baptism?

4. Would you say you have tended to be at either of the extremes we described? That is, have you tended on the one hand to make baptism a very marginal issue, or on the other hand have you tended to make it the major issue?

5. What would be a more balanced view?

# 2

# BAPTISM AND GRACE

I would like to take you behind the scenes and talk about the formation of this book. I often have people ask me how books come together. I'm not sure you are wondering about this, but I'm going to share a little bit with you.

I considered several options for this chapter. My desire, of course, was to connect with you as the reader. I was not just interested in laying out a lot of information, but wanted to invite you along on a little trip that could have much value.

I had to face the fact that this is a subject that many people have not thought of as being exciting, but even more so, it is one that readers of this book will already have quite definite ideas about.

At one stage I thought that it would only make sense to begin with "Baptism and Faith" since (1) faith is such a crucial quality in all aspects of the spiritual life, (2) baptism and faith are sometimes, mistakenly, set against one another, and (3) the Reformation concept of "faith alone" is often viewed as something much different from what the reformers had in mind.

For a while I seriously considered beginning with "Baptism and the Kingdom," for reasons I hope will become obvious in the next chapter. At the same time, I considered putting this chapter, which is on grace, at the end of the book. As Paul says that love binds together all the essential qualities of the Spirit-filled life in perfect harmony (Colossians 3:14), I could see grace binding together all the various meanings of baptism and thus providing a fitting conclusion.

### God's Glorious Grace

However, in the end, because there is so much misunderstanding about the relationship between grace and baptism in the Christian world, I decided that we must start here. And then we will let faith be that quality that binds together the various elements.

I begin with grace because I am concerned that there be no doubt and no fuzziness or lack of clarity about my posture in this book. *We are saved by grace*. We have God's

Kingdom by grace. We are part of God's chosen and elect people by grace. Everything about the new life comes *because of* and *by God's grace*.

It is hard to put too much emphasis on grace. I am just not sure that we can. We can distort grace or misuse grace, but I am not sure it can be overemphasized, and reading the letter to the Ephesians would lead me to that conclusion. Listen to Paul's words:

> Praise be to the God and Father of our Lord Jesus Christ, who has blessed us in the heavenly realms with every spiritual blessing in Christ. For he chose us in him before the creation of the world to be holy and blameless in his sight. In love he predestined us for adoption to sonship through Jesus Christ, in accordance with his pleasure and will—to the praise of his glorious grace, which he has freely given us in the One he loves. In him we have redemption through his blood, the forgiveness of sins, in accordance with the riches of God's grace that he lavished on us. (Ephesians 1:3–8)

God's grace is glorious and, of course, by very definition, freely given. It is to be praised. God is to be honored for it. God has *riches* of grace, and out of those riches, he *lavishes* grace on us. Try to grasp this. There are people who are incredibly rich, and out of their riches they lavish gifts on those they favor. But God is the richest of all, and he is rich in grace or astonishing generosity.

Now think of the word "lavish." It is the Greek word *eperisseusen*. It means "over and above, going further and beyond, exceeding all expectations." We have likely heard stories of people with great riches going over the top in their generosity usually to a lover or sometimes to a child, but what does it look like when God lavishes, when he goes way beyond all expectations? Whatever it looks like, it is superabundantly more than any man can ever do.

This is what leads me to say that I don't think we can overemphasize grace. It has a height and depth and length and width that I doubt any of us have understood or will understand (compare Ephesians 3:18–19). No wonder Paul says, "Praise be to God." Every blessing we enjoy comes from God's costly, superabundant and lavish grace.

### Baptism and God's Grace

Professor G.R. Beasley-Murray, the well-known British scholar, in his classic study of baptism, writes,

> The extent and nature of the grace which the New Testament writers declare to be present in baptism is astonishing for any who come to the study freshly with an open mind.[1]

He follows this with a list of sixteen gifts and blessings

---

1. G.R. Beasley-Murray, *Baptism in the New Testament* (Grand Rapids: Eerdmans, 1962, reprinted 1994), 263.

that come to us in connection with baptism. Then he asks:

> How are we to explain this attribution of the fullness of saving grace to the performance of an outward act like baptism?[2]

With this question he is raising the issue we want to address in this chapter: What is the relationship of grace and baptism, and what does it mean for living the baptized life?

In spite of all the connections between baptism and God's grace that a scholar like Beasley-Murray finds in an open-minded reading of the New Testament, there are many who are extremely opposed to thinking there is any connection between baptism and the receiving of grace, baptism and salvation, or baptism and forgiveness.

In spite of all we have said at the beginning of this chapter about the primacy of grace, there are those who feel that to bring baptism into the discussion is basically to nullify everything we have said about grace. For them, to be saved by grace is to allow nothing else into the picture, although you will find disagreement among these folks as to whether faith and repentance should be included.

However, they would all agree that an "outward act" like baptism can play no part in a plan that involves salvation by grace, except to say that baptism eventually needs

2. Beasley-Murray, *Baptism*, 264.

to be done as "an outward sign of an inward grace" (a grace that has already been given to a person before baptism and separate and apart from baptism).

The role of baptism, then, is to be just a testimony to grace that has already done its work and has already made the person new. Baptism in this view is not a place of receiving grace, but a place in which you tell of an already received grace to others. Some of you may very well have viewed it this way, or, perhaps, still do. But let me invite you to examine the relationship between grace and baptism in the Scriptures.

### Grace Is More Important

First, let us be clear that if we are comparing grace and baptism, we are looking at two things that are most unequal. God's grace, as it comes to us through Jesus Christ, is the more important of the two by far, for it has a reality all its own, is displayed in so many ways, and issues the call to baptism. Grace gives baptism the only meaning it has.

Having said that, we must realize that we are creating a false dichotomy if we face off grace against baptism. That would be akin to lining up a fireman against his hose or a surgeon against his scalpel. Certainly in each case one is the greater and one is the lesser, but there is foolishness is setting one over against the other.

A text in Paul's letter to Titus that references both grace and baptism gives us some important insights into the relationship of the two:

> At one time we too were foolish, disobedient, deceived and enslaved by all kinds of passions and pleasures. We lived in malice and envy, being hated and hating one another. But when the kindness and love of God our Savior appeared, he saved us, not because of righteous things we had done, but because of his mercy. He saved us through the washing of rebirth and renewal by the Holy Spirit, whom he poured out on us generously through Jesus Christ our Savior, so that, having been justified by his grace, we might become heirs having the hope of eternal life. This is a trustworthy saying. And I want you to stress these things, so that those who have trusted in God may be careful to devote themselves to doing what is good. These things are excellent and profitable for everyone. (Titus 3:3–8)

Man's condition apart from Christ is clearly described: foolish, disobedient, deceived and enslaved. Into this dark picture breaks the kindness and love of God *our Savior*, who saves us, clearly not because of righteous things we have done.

The saving work is all his, done through the washing

of rebirth and renewal by the Holy Spirit. "The washing of rebirth" is reminiscent of John 3 and being born again of the water and the Spirit, of Acts 2 and being called to baptism for forgiveness of sin and the gift of the Spirit, of Acts 22 when Paul hears "get up, be baptized and wash away your sins," and of Romans 6 where one is buried with Christ in baptism and rises to be a new person. The word baptism does not occur in this passage from Titus, but because of these parallels almost all exegetes who are not trying to defend some theological position are in agreement that Paul is making a reference to baptism.

But it is most important that all of this is summed up with the phrase *"having been justified by his grace."* Baptism is not in the category of "righteous things we had done" but is one of the elements through which God brings us his grace, which justifies us. As we look more closely in the rest of this chapter, we will see why baptism belongs in the "grace box" and not in the "righteous things box."

### Give All Credit to God

It seems to me that there are at least three takeaways from the Titus 3 passage. First, living the baptized life means we will want to leave no doubt in anyone's mind as to the source of our salvation and justification. All the credit goes to God, his grace and his generosity.

In baptism it is God doing the washing, the regenerating and the renewing. The construction of the Greek text in verse 5 is such that the Holy Spirit should be seen as both doing the washing of rebirth and the renewing. Since baptism may look more to others like something we are doing, it behooves us to take extra care to stress to those being baptized and those observing a baptism that this is all God's work.

I must tell you that in the fellowship I am part of, I hear certain language that bothers me. I hear a good many people say things such as, "He is going to get baptized tonight" or "I got baptized last Saturday" or "I got baptized about a week before my wife was ready to." You may see nothing wrong with such comments, but it is the words "get" and "got" that trouble me. Besides the fact that the Scriptures never use such language, there is the fact that these verbs leave more the impression that baptism is *something we do*.

When we say that friend James *got* rich investing in real estate, we usually are referring to his accomplishments. The same would be true of friend Sarah who went back to school to *get* her degree. After she acquired the sheepskin, we might say she *got* her degree in 2013. We even say that friend Logan and his fiancée Maria *got* married last June, referring to something they did.

On the negative side, we speak of a person who went out and *got* drunk, communicating that he made the decision to do so and is responsible for what happens. But you may wonder what the problem is. Isn't baptism something we do?

In one very important sense, the answer is no. Baptism is much more what God does (as Father, Son and Spirit) than it is something we do. And some of us need to have our thinking changed at this point. Baptism is a place of grace and not a place of our "doing." Biblically this is seen in the fact that baptism is almost always spoken of in *the passive voice*—meaning baptism is something done to us.

This is true on two levels. Physically we place ourselves in someone else's hands, and they immerse us, but that is demonstrating or representing a deeper spiritual truth: We place ourselves in the hands of God who immerses us into Christ. Notice just some of the many examples we find in the New Testament, with emphasis added:

- Peter replied, "Repent and *be* baptized…. (passive voice) (Acts 2:38)

- …they *were* baptized, both men and women. (passive voice) (Acts 8:12)

- For we *were* all baptized by one Spirit into one body—whether Jews or Greeks, slave or free—and we were all given the one Spirit to drink. (passive voice with God's Spirit doing the baptizing) (1 Corinthians 12:13)

- Or don't you know that all of us who *were* baptized into Christ Jesus *were* baptized into his death? (passive voice) (Romans 6:3)

- We *were* therefore buried with him through baptism into death in order that, just as Christ was raised from the dead through the glory of the Father, we too may live a new life. (passive voice) (Romans 6:4)

We are not being picky here. We are just taking note that the writers are very particular about the verb voice they select and that it is the passive voice that indicates baptism is not something "we do" but something that is done to us. Of course, like the lepers who came to Jesus, we must recognize our need and come to him for help, but having done that, we must confess that we do not have the power to kill an old life, bury it and raise up a new life. Only God can do that.

There may not seem to be much difference in someone who "got baptized" and someone who "was baptized," but the biblical writers consistently choose the passive voice, and I am convinced it is for a reason. We surrender ourselves to him, lay down all our claims, confess our need and allow him to do what only he can do. Because it is biblically correct and because there is so much misunderstanding in the religious world, we should continually emphasize this is *something God has done.*

In this regard, it would be much better and much more biblical not to say things like "I got baptized twenty-seven years ago," but rather "Twenty-seven years ago I was baptized," or even "Twenty-seven years ago I was united with Christ in baptism and was raised up by the power of God." Using the passive voice and being more descriptive is spiritually correct and healthy. I understand our preference for verbal shorthand, but when it comes to something so important, wouldn't it be good (for others, as well as for ourselves) to use a few more words to make it clear that the glory does not belong to us but to him? What happens in baptism is all God's doing.

All the things we are going to see in the following chapters are "to the praise of his glorious grace, which he has freely given us in the One he loves" (Ephesians 1:6). The reason Paul could passionately write about being saved by grace in Romans 1–5 and then move seamlessly into an emphasis on what happens to us in baptism in Romans 6 is because he saw that what occurs in baptism is an expression of God's grace.

This is also the reason he could, in Galatians 1–3, challenge any theology that relied on human effort and not God's Spirit, and then say at the end of all that: "You are all sons of God through faith in Christ Jesus, for all of you who were baptized into Christ have clothed yourselves with Christ" (Galatians 3:26–27). Had he seen baptism as some good work—some expression of human effort—that we might be tempted to rely on, this is the last place he would have wanted to bring it up. But, for Paul, you never line up baptism against grace. What happens in baptism is all about grace.

### *Fully Enjoy God's Grace*

Second, I would suggest we need to fully enjoy God's generous grace. Maybe the word *luxuriate* in it is the right idea if we understand this in its primary meaning, which is "to grow profusely or to thrive." Paul told Timothy,

> Command those who are rich in this present world not to be arrogant nor to put their hope in wealth, which is so uncertain, but to put their hope in God, who richly provides us with everything for our enjoyment. (1 Timothy 6:17)

If God has provided us food, drink, beauty and friendship for our enjoyment, surely he has lavished his grace on us spiritually for our enjoyment. Grace is not just a doctrine; it is a state we live in. It is an atmosphere we breathe in. We have been plunged into it. We are swimming in it and being refreshed by it.

Robert Webber, in describing the meaning of baptism, relates a story I find helpful in thinking this through, as well as a story I just enjoy repeating!

Baptism is best expressed with lots of water, to a lavish use of it splashing and flying everywhere so there is no missing the point. For in baptism we are plunged and immersed into Jesus Christ, who restores God's creatures and creation as we stay in the waters bathed in God's perpetual grace.

I am told that in some African indigenous church many are baptized in the ocean. New converts are taken to the shoreline where deacons pick them up by the hands and feet, swing them in the air, then throw them into a wave in the name of the Father. When they have rolled back on the shore, the deacons pick them up and throw them into another wave in the name of the Son. And then a third time, in the name of the Spirit. I have it on good report that this is true.

This ocean baptismal tradition is a great illustration of our being willingly plunged into the waters of baptism where God's creative power to restore us to himself by the work of his two hands is manifested in a material way. The proper response is "get me to that water; throw me in; get me immersed in it. I want that water to rush all over me, around me, and through me. I want to be identified with Jesus, the one through whom I have been embraced by God."[3]

If this account makes you want to engage in some holy laughter, go right ahead. I can just picture the congregation

---

3. Webber, *The Divine Embrace*, 159.

on the shore cheering each time the person goes under. There is a happy celebratory spirit here that seems just right. This unusual baptismal practice and Webber's comments about it seem to capture the biblical connection of grace and baptism.

As we are plunged into an abundance of water that can immerse us and enclose us, so we are plunged into an abundance of grace. Wave after wave of it keeps coming, and all to give us life, love, strength and, yes, enjoyment. Living the baptized life means continuing to see a flood of God's grace coming our way. It means an end to all efforts to justify ourselves so we can enjoy that we are sons and daughters of God by grace.

Think of children playing in a backyard swimming pool. See them cupping their hands and sending a spray onto their friends. See them diving down and hiding and then emerging with a shout. Now try to see yourself at play in God's pool of grace, humbly enjoying the moments like a little child.

### Never Abuse God's Grace

Finally, while grace should be celebrated and enjoyed, it is not to be abused. God's work is to create new people in Christ Jesus who will devote themselves to doing what is good (Titus 3:8). Trusting God's grace never means thinking we now have freedom to sin, but rather that we have been freed from sin. Earlier in Titus 2 Paul made a similar point:

> For the grace of God that brings salvation has appeared to all men. It teaches us to say "No" to ungodliness and worldly passions, and to live self-controlled, upright and godly lives in this present age. (vv11–12)

Both of these texts in Titus are parallel to Paul's words in Ephesians 2:

> For it is by grace you have been saved, through faith—and this not from yourselves, it is the gift of God—not by works, so that no one can boast. For we are God's workmanship, created in Christ Jesus to do good works, which God prepared in advance for us to do. (vv8–10)

First comes grace, received by faith. (In a later chapter, we will look at Galatians 3:26–27 where faith and baptism are united.) This creates us in Christ for work God has planned in advance. Anyone who does not want the new life and the new work doesn't really want or trust the grace that produces such things. Why would they, since grace brings a lot more than forgiveness?

The baptized life is one of gratitude, but also serious commitment—the commitment to be gracious to the poor as God has been gracious to us, to be graceful to the sinful and lost as God has been graceful to us, to be loving toward our enemies as God loved us while we were his enemies, and to forgive those who sin against us as God has forgiven us. As we splash and frolic in the waters of grace, we want that grace to spill out of our pool and into the lives of others. Out of baptism we are always emerging to serve. Grace has transformed us. A life that is immersed in Jesus looks more and more like Jesus.

*But we, little fishes after the example of our Ichthus (ΙΧΘΥΣ), Jesus Christ, are born in water, nor have we safety in any other way than by permanently abiding in water…*

## Questions for
## Study and Discussion

1. Why is there the tendency among many to put grace and baptism in different categories?

2. What are the reasons for considering baptism to be something that God does more than something we do? How persuaded are you that this is the correct way to think?

3. How can those who see the importance of baptism show to others that salvation is primarily by grace?

4. What thoughts do you have about enjoying God's grace? Is this something easy or difficult for you?

5. What do you take away from this chapter about living the baptized life?

# 3

# BAPTISM
# AND
# THE KINGDOM

Jesus spoke about many things, but he had one central message: *The Kingdom of God has arrived.* This was a proclamation that both resonated with and confused those who heard him. It resonated with the Jewish people because they had been anticipating the Kingdom of God coming in power for a long time, and their ears perked up when someone with unique qualities and charisma said that it was here.

However, his preaching confused them because Jesus acted like the Kingdom was coming right in the middle of the present age, when most of them believed the coming of the Kingdom would mean the end of the present world and the inauguration of the age to come.

In Jesus' teaching, the coming of the Kingdom meant a whole new order of life was breaking into the present world. True enough, Jesus taught that there was still a fullness of the Kingdom that was "not yet" and would come at the end of the present age. But the reign and rule of God was being seen "already" in the life of Jesus.

Furthermore, the Kingdom would be seen in the lives of all those who became his disciples. This meant it would be evident in this community that Jesus called his *ecclesia*, a word we usually translate as "church." This was a word that referred to a group called out to a unique life or special purpose.

Indeed, other passages in the New Testament will tell us these disciples understood that their identity had so changed that their real citizenship was in heaven (Philippians 3:20). Consequently, their distinctiveness would be so great that it would draw the ire of those around them, who would often treat them as strangers and aliens in this world (1 Peter 2:11).

### Baptisma: What Does It Mean?

What does the act of baptism have to do with such a great concept as the Kingdom? We will address that momentarily, but first let's take note of this word "baptism." We speak today of baptism, instead of immersion, because four or five hundred years ago English translators decided to *transliterate* the Greek word instead of *translating* it. Not surprisingly, there was some political pressure to do this.

Sprinkling had become the dominant practice of the state church, and to render *baptisma* as immersion (which it literally means) would have been an embarrassment to the religious powers.

Their decision contributed to the confusion that has been part of the ongoing discussion of this important event in people's lives. For the most part in this book, we will use the terms baptism or baptize (instead of immersion and immerse) because that is the terminology we are accustomed to, but we should keep in mind the primary meaning of the original Greek.

### Turning Point Baptism

To return to the connection between baptism and the Kingdom, we must actually start with someone who came before Jesus and who was the first to announce the coming of the Kingdom. We are referring, of course, to John, interestingly named the Baptizer (or John the Immerser). John was not only the first one to announce that the Kingdom of God was arriving (Matthew 3:2) but also the first to call people to what we might describe as a "turning point baptism."

The Scriptures tell us that John begins preaching in the Judean desert saying, "Repent, for the kingdom of heaven is near" (Matthew 3:2). Along with this he was "preaching a baptism of repentance for the forgiveness of sins" (Mark 1:4).

Immersions of various kinds were a common experience in Judaism both as they were practiced in Jerusalem by traditional leaders and by the sectarians known as the Essenes. The latter had given up on current-day Judaism because of what they saw as the corruption of the Temple and had retired to the area we know as Qumran near the Dead Sea.

However, with both these cases in Judaism, immersion was something repeated often and thus is more properly viewed as "lustrations" or ceremonial washings. Josephus, the Jewish historian, implies that members of the Essene community would undergo immersion three times a day—morning, mid-day and evening.[1] John's baptism was altogether different.

John was not introducing another practice of repeated immersion but a "turning point" baptism (or a conversion baptism). It was a baptism of repentance—an immersion of those accepting a radical change, an immersion that would do more than make a person ceremonially clean, but would actually bring God's gift of the forgiveness of sins to the one who was committing himself or herself to a new way of life. When one was baptized by John, he most certainly did not get up the next morning and say, "I need to do this again today," (or three times today). No, he more likely would have thought or said, "I need to remember what was done yesterday and live it today."

---

1. *Wars of the Jews*, II, vii.5, 9.

## Baptism and the Kingdom of God

As the news of John spread, great numbers went out into the desert to hear his preaching, respond to his call, and prepare for the coming Kingdom by receiving his baptism.

With his popularity growing, with the attention of the crowds focused on him, and with incredible personal power within his grasp, John did not follow normal human instinct. Instead, he embraced God's plan and humbled himself. He said, "After me will come one who is more powerful than I, whose sandals I am not fit to carry" (Matthew 3:11b).

With Jesus not yet on the scene, John called people to not focus on him, but on the one coming later. John was already demonstrating the most essential quality of the coming Kingdom—humility.

Jesus saw John's work as a unique and decisive moment for Israel and for him, and he, too, went to John. Jesus and John were on the same kingdom page, though John could only see partially what Jesus could see. And so we read:

> Then Jesus came from Galilee to the Jordan to be baptized by John. But John tried to deter him, saying, "I need to be baptized by you, and do you come to me?"

> Jesus replied, "Let it be so now; it is proper for us
> to do this to fulfill all righteousness." Then John con-
> sented. (Matthew 3:13–15)

With the crowds streaming out, Jesus joins them, and
most likely, stands in line with all the others with the desire
to place his body in John's hands for immersion. And here,
in Jesus, we see it again—kingdom humility. He is not
threatened by John. He has no desire to compete. He
comes to submit to God through John.

Jesus' turn comes. He stands before John. The desert
prophet, to some extent, understands the moment and rec-
ognizes the one before him. He says to Jesus, in so many
words, "This is not the right thing. I need to receive baptism from you" (Matthew 3:15a). When Jesus explains, in
humility, that John must immerse him, *John submits to Jesus'
submission* (3:15b). Surely Satan hated it. Humility was on
all sides. Quietly, but powerfully, the Kingdom was breaking in.

But what are we to make of Jesus' baptism and the
statement, "It is proper for us to do this to fulfill all righteousness"? The most superficial understanding of this
would be to say that this was another requirement God
had added, and that fulfilling all righteousness meant Jesus
had to check that box off his "to do" list. Sadly, this is the
way many people view this statement, and then they carry

that thinking over into their understanding about baptism in their own lives.

We have already noted that John's baptism was far more than a requirement. It was a "moment" especially charged with meaning and significance. It represented a turning point. Though this baptism could not have meant for Jesus exactly what it meant for others, why do some so quickly think that it meant *less*? Given Jesus' understanding of the drama that God was playing out in his life, we have all the reason in the world to think that his baptism meant *not less but more*. Please pardon the pun, but in Jesus' baptism we are in deep water. Scholars for years have sought to explore these waters, and, yet, surely no one has all the answers. But consider these thoughts:

1. *The response to Jesus' baptism by God the Father shows this was a momentous event.* As Jesus came rising up out of the water, "at that moment heaven was opened, and he saw the Spirit of God descending like a dove and lighting on him. And a voice from heaven said, 'This is my Son, whom I love; with him I am well pleased'" (Matthew 3:16–17).

Only three times in the New Testament are we told of God's voice coming from heaven: here, on the Mount of Transfiguration, and in the events described in John 12 when Jesus committed to go and die. What is important enough to cause heaven to open, for the Holy Spirit to descend "like a dove…lighting on him," for God to declare, "This is my boy. I love him and am pleased with him"? Apparently a baptism! In this case Jesus' baptism.

One finds believers who say the primary reason to be baptized is to follow the example of Jesus. However, it is ironic that this thinking usually goes hand in hand with a view that baptism plays a peripheral role in one's spiritual life. It is part of the "requirement thinking" that says, "Jesus did it and so I need to do it." But, most often to such people one's baptism becomes a mere footnote to the life in Christ, since most everything of significance is found somewhere else.

Whatever we want to say about Jesus' baptism, it was not just an earth-shattering event, but a heaven-shattering event as well. That day when Jesus went down into the water, was buried in baptism, and was raised up by John was big, significant and bursting with meaning. Heaven's fireworks went off immediately. The Spirit came rushing down. God boomed his approval.

There are differences in our baptism and the baptism of Jesus, but, as we will see, in both cases something monumental has happened. If that does not fit with our teaching and understanding, some significant correction is needed.

2. *In being baptized Jesus did something crucial to advance the Kingdom.* This is the only conclusion we can draw from the first point we just made. Jesus was all about the Kingdom. His subsequent preaching makes that clear. God was using him to bring the Kingdom into the present age. Therefore, this explosive response to his baptism means he had taken the first giant step toward fulfilling that goal.

But why was Jesus baptized? Why was he so determined to let it happen? Why did the Father respond with unprecedented approval? John's preaching was to prepare for one coming after him. He preached a baptism of repentance for the forgiveness of sins. If you or I were writing the script, we likely would decide that since Jesus was the one John's preaching was preparing everyone for and since we subsequently learn Jesus did not need to repent or to be forgiven of sin, there would be no need for him to come to the Jordan and be immersed. But man's ways are not God's ways.

The Messiah would not marshal the patriots of Israel and lead them against the foreigners. Neither would he opt out of baptism because of his superior position. In the spirit of Isaiah 53 (which was so perplexing and misunderstood by the Jewish people), Jesus would enter into the world of those who were lost in the darkness of sin and inaugurate his ministry by joining them in baptism. He who knew no sin would begin the process of bearing the sin of others by humbling himself before the preacher of repentance and baptism.

Jesus' baptism made a statement. But here is an often overlooked fact: His baptism represented a choice made out his freedom. Logic surely tempted him to avoid looking like just another member of "the great unwashed." Why should he? But a kingdom focus moved him to put himself among them and begin the journey to a cross where he would, in Isaiah's words, be "pierced for our transgressions" and "crushed for our iniquities." The great unwashed needed cleansing, and to bring this to them, Jesus needed to plunge with them into the water of baptism.

The Kingdom would turn all man's thinking upside down. In seeking and submitting to baptism, Jesus was freely choosing the kingdom path of complete humility, and continuing the prophetic practice of bringing the truth of God not just with words but actions.

In baptism Jesus made a statement. And then God made a statement. But then something else also came from God. Actually someone else came from God, and that was his Spirit, the Holy Spirit that came like a dove and lit on Jesus. While John did not preach a baptism that would bring the Spirit, this is exactly who came to Jesus. This action not only showed God's endorsement of Jesus, but demonstrated that God's power would be with him. Significantly for us, it also foreshadowed the gift of the Spirit that would soon accompany baptism in the name of Jesus. We will look at the Spirit and baptism in chapter 7.

After the inauguration of Jesus' ministry, what would be the ongoing role of immersion in water? John had said, "I baptize you with water for repentance. But after me will come one who is more powerful than I, whose sandals I am not fit to carry. He will baptize you with the Holy Spirit and with fire" (Matthew 3:11).

Did this mean that Jesus' baptism was a fulfillment that brought this practice to an end? Would immersion going forward no longer be a physical act but now an experience of being overwhelmed by the Holy Spirit and a fiery zeal (or perhaps, a fiery judgment for those who rejected the Kingdom)?

There is no hint that Jesus' baptism ended the practice of baptizing in water. To the contrary, the fourth Gospel tells us that both John's disciples and those of Jesus continued to immerse new followers (John 3:22–27, 4:1–3).

There has been considerable discussion and speculation about the relationship of John's baptism and that practiced by Jesus' disciples before his death and resurrection. Were the two the same, or was there something distinctive about baptism in Jesus' ministry? Given the scarcity of material, we simply do not know. All we can say is that these two

men who were simultaneously heralding the coming Kingdom were calling people to submit to baptism as a meaningful act that was somehow relating them and connecting
them to the breaking in of the age to come.

What is most interesting and instructive is that the two
references to the continuation of baptism in the ministry
of John and Jesus come just after a most important teaching in the Gospel of John about entering the Kingdom. We
must examine these words from John 3:

> Now there was a man of the Pharisees named
> Nicodemus, a member of the Jewish ruling council.
> He came to Jesus at night and said, "Rabbi, we know
> you are a teacher who has come from God. For no
> one could perform the miraculous signs you are
> doing if God were not with him."
>
> In reply Jesus declared, "I tell you the truth, no
> one can see the kingdom of God unless he is born
> again."
>
> "How can a man be born when he is old?" Nicode-
> mus asked. "Surely he cannot enter a second time
> into his mother's womb to be born!"
>
> Jesus answered, "I tell you the truth, no one can
> enter the kingdom of God unless he is born of water
> and the Spirit. Flesh gives birth to flesh, but the Spirit
> gives birth to spirit. You should not be surprised at
> my saying, 'You must be born again.'" (John 3:1–7)

In John 3 and the opening verses of John 4, then, this is what we find:

1. Jesus has a discussion with a leading Pharisee who approaches him, surprisingly, to affirm his teaching and ministry. Jesus brings up the subject of the Kingdom of God and tells Nicodemus no one can enter it unless he experiences a new birth (or maybe more accurately, a birth from above). When Nicodemus questions how this can happen, Jesus answers that one must be born of water and the Spirit in order to enter the Kingdom.

2. Comments on these events and the nature of Jesus' work are added apparently by John, the Gospel writer.

3. Then, in this context, we read "After this, Jesus and his disciples went out into the Judean countryside, where he spent some time with them, and baptized" (v22).

4. We are told that John was continuing his ministry and baptizing because he had not yet been imprisoned (vv23–24).

5. Certain Jews are described who seem perplexed about the relationship of John's work and that of Jesus, apparently wondering if Jesus' ministry is going to supplant John's (vv25–26).

6. John humbly replies, "A man can only receive what is given him from heaven" (v27), and then goes further to say, "He must become greater and I must become less" (v30).

7. The section ends in the first three verses of chapter 4, where the Pharisees take note that a greater number of

baptisms are being seen in Jesus' ministry than John's, and Jesus decides to go somewhere else, apparently to avoid any hint of competition.

## New Birth into the Kingdom

Whether Nicodemus views Jesus as the expected Messiah, we cannot be sure. He does view him as one come from God. Jesus uses the occasion to bring up a topic Nicodemus had no doubt often studied and discussed. As a practicing member of one of the more devoted Jewish groups, he would have certainly expected that he would be part of the coming Kingdom of God.

However, he hears he will not enter it unless he experiences a new birth—a new birth that Jesus quickly says is one "of water and the Spirit."

After the discussion, Nicodemus likely saw what John's Gospel goes on to describe: a growing Kingdom of God movement that involved numerous baptisms both by John's ministry and by that of Jesus. It is worth mentioning that church leaders of the second and third centuries were united in understanding that "born of water" in John 3 referred to baptism.[2]

The Kingdom was breaking in. John the Baptizer introduced it. In Jesus it was being seen. Now Jesus teaches

---

2. Included in this group would be Justin Martyr ("First Apology," *Ante-Nicene Fathers, vol. 1,* page 183), Clement ("Recognitions of Clement," *Ante-Nicene Fathers, vol. 8,* page 155), Theophilus of Antioch (To Autolycus 12:16), and Cyprian (Letters 71[72]:1).

that it is such a different order of life that no one could share it (and live it) without a new birth—a birth from above, a birth from the new age. That new birth would come through submission to God in the water of baptism and in reception of the Holy Spirit. If this is not perfectly clear, it will become so in subsequent texts, particularly in the Book of Acts. As we have already pointed out, Paul would later describe it this way: "He saved us through the washing of rebirth and renewal by the Holy Spirit, whom he poured out on us generously through Jesus Christ our Savior" (Titus 3:5b–6).

Baptism plays a vital role not only in the inauguration of Jesus' kingdom ministry and in the midst of his ministry, but also in his marching orders after his death and resurrection. Of all four Gospels, Matthew has more emphasis on Jesus' kingdom message. His book closes with these well-known words:

> Then Jesus came to them and said, "All authority in heaven and on earth has been given to me. Therefore go and make disciples of all nations, baptizing them in the name of the Father and of the Son and of the Holy Spirit, and teaching them to obey everything I have commanded you. And surely I am with you always, to the very end of the age." (Matthew 28:18–20)

In this charge, which we usually call the Great Commission, Jesus echoes something he had said before his death: "And this gospel of the kingdom will be preached in the whole world as a testimony to all nations, and then the end will come" (Matthew 24:14).

In his kingdom ministry Jesus is fulfilling everything said to Abraham, Isaac and Jacob about their offspring being a blessing to all peoples on earth. God had longed for Israel to be that, but now Jesus is the Israel God always wanted. Now Jesus, who has suffered that all might come to God, sends his disciples to preach the gospel of the Kingdom to all nations. Given what we have already studied, it should not surprise us that the charge to make disciples should include the command to baptize. And we are told this is to be done in the name of the Father, and of the Son and of the Holy Spirit.

Immediately we may think that this means when one is baptized we need to be sure that the right words or formula is used. Right words are fine and good, but this concern is probably missing the point. Both in Hebrew and Greek cultures "in the name of" had significant and quite related meanings. Combining the shades of meaning, we might say, to be baptized in the name of Father, Son and Spirit meant one was being baptized in respect of the Father, for the sake of the Son, and to be in relationship to the Spirit, as well to belong to God, submit to the Son, and show the ownership of the Spirit.

All of this is to say that baptism is relational not mechanical. Baptism is not so much about doing something with the right words and forms as it is about doing something that brings one into a new relationship with the triune God—a relationship in which we have surrendered control to him as Father, Son and Spirit. To be baptized in response to the good news of the Kingdom is to place oneself under the reign of God and to fully belong to the real King.

So, what does it mean to live the baptized life? It is to…

- Live the kingdom life.
- Live as a citizen of heaven.
- Live as an alien and a stranger in this world.
- Pledge allegiance to only one King and one holy nation.
- Commit to "obeying everything [he] commanded" (Matthew 28:20).
- Embrace kingdom attitudes such as poverty of spirit, meekness and purity of heart.
- Overcome evil with good, and love one's enemies.
- Lay up treasures in heaven not on the earth.
- Care for the poor.
- Be involved in making disciples of all nations.

To live the baptized life is to pray, "Father, your Kingdom come, your will be done on earth as it is in heaven."

*There is no story but God's;*
*no God but the Father, Son and Spirit;*
*and no life but the baptized life.*

## Questions for
## Study and Discussion

1. What ideas have you had in the past about why Jesus came to be baptized by John?

2. What meaning should we attach to the fact that God the Father gives such a strong affirmation to Jesus' baptism? Particularly, what meaning should this have for us?

3. What new ideas did you find in this chapter, and what are your thoughts about them?

4. If you were asked to explain the connection between the Kingdom of God and baptism, what would you say?

5. What normal ways of living are challenged by the idea of living the kingdom life?

**4**

# BAPTISM AND SALVATION

Jesus taught how the new life of the Kingdom of God could be lived out in this present age. If one were to listen to much preaching in "Bible centered" churches today, he or she would very likely come away with the impression that just about all Jesus talked about was receiving forgiveness of sin so you could go to heaven when you die. One would hear little about the Kingdom.

While an overemphasis on being forgiven so you can go to heaven would be very misleading, the message of salvation *was* a significant element in his teaching, part of his gospel of the Kingdom, and certainly a theme in the rest of the New Testament.

### The Meaning of Salvation

When the New Testament speaks of salvation, we must

bear in mind that it does not always mean salvation from sin, as is apparent in a passage about Jesus early in Luke:

> "He has raised up a horn of salvation for us in the house of his servant David (as he said through his holy prophets of long ago), salvation from our ene-mies and from the hand of all who hate us." (Luke 1:69–71)

"Salvation" is another word for "deliverance" as is clearly the meaning in this passage, and it may be deliverance from such things as enemies, slavery, bondage or trial. "Saved" is certainly used in this broader sense at the time of the cruci-fixion when Jesus is mocked by his executioners:

> The people stood watching, and the rulers even sneered at him. They said, "He saved others; let him save himself if he is the Christ of God, the Chosen One."
>
> The soldiers also came up and mocked him. They offered him wine vinegar and said, "If you are the king of the Jews, save yourself."(Luke 23:35–37)

However, there is no doubting that salvation or deliv-erance from sin is clearly in mind as we hear the words of the angel to Zachariah, the father of John the Baptizer:

> "And you, my child, will be called a prophet of the Most High; for you will go on before the Lord to

> prepare the way for him, to give his people the knowledge of salvation through the forgiveness of their sins." (Luke 1:76–77)

Salvation in this text is certainly linked with forgiveness of sins, though not totally equated with it. Matthew's Gospel records words spoken to Joseph by another angel that make this connection even clearer.

> "She will give birth to a son, and you are to give him the name Jesus, because he will save his people from their sins." (Matthew 1:21)

We cannot say that the Jewish expectations of the Kingdom focused much on the forgiveness of sins or salvation from sin. For the most part, it seems the Jews saw themselves as on God's side, and they were just waiting for him to break in and bring deliverance from their oppressors and give them the place he always intended for them to have.

But we can see from these angelic announcements that God linked the coming Kingdom with forgiveness of sins, which was a genuine need. Only when this happened could people enjoy a relationship with him under his rule and reign.

All of this fits with the Baptizer's preaching, described this way first by Mark:

> And so John came, baptizing in the desert region and preaching a baptism of repentance for the forgiveness of sins. The whole Judean countryside and all the people of Jerusalem went out to him. Confessing their sins, they were baptized by him in the Jordan River. (Mark 1:4–5)

The proclamation of the Kingdom is accompanied by a call to a baptism described as one "of repentance" and "for the forgiveness of sins." As we saw in chapter 3, this preaching is soon endorsed by Jesus who himself requests the baptism from John.

Toward the beginning of his ministry Jesus speaks of the forgiveness of sins when healing the paralyzed man who was brought to Jesus by his friends. Though none of them seemed to have come seeking it, "Your sins are forgiven" are Jesus' first words to the man. Then he goes on to bring healing to those motionless legs to make it clear that "the Son of Man has authority on earth to forgive sins" (Mark 2:10).

Later to the sinful woman, who anointed Jesus' feet with her tears and dried them with her hair, he said: "Your sins are forgiven" (Luke 7:48). The Kingdom is about many things, certainly including forgiveness, salvation and deliverance from sin.

And so after the resurrection, the risen Jesus tells the men on the road to Emmaus:

> "This is what is written: The Christ will suffer and rise from the dead on the third day, and repentance and forgiveness of sins will be preached in his name to all nations, beginning at Jerusalem." (Luke 24:46–47)

When John had preached a baptism of repentance for the forgiveness of sins, he apparently was preaching mostly to Jews, but now Jesus makes it clear that the long-standing promise of the prophets will be fulfilled: The Gentiles will be included. His word of forgiveness will go to all nations.

### Baptism in the Name of Jesus

The fact that baptism seems to disappear from the story after the early chapters of the Gospels and is not referred to in these final words in Luke might cause one to wonder if the act had served its purpose during a transitional time. However, we have already seen how the command by the resurrected Jesus to make disciples and baptize them brought Matthew's Gospel to an end.

And then, as soon as we are into the Book of Acts, which records the continuation of Jesus' ministry through the Holy Spirit and the apostles, it is Luke who not only describes the call to baptism, but shows baptism's clear connection to the forgiveness of sins.

Consider the conclusion to Peter's sermon in Acts 2:

"Therefore let all Israel be assured of this: God has made this Jesus, whom you crucified, both Lord and Christ." When the people heard this, they were cut to the heart and said to Peter and the other apostles, "Brothers, what shall we do?"

Peter replied, "Repent and be baptized, every one of you, in the name of Jesus Christ for the forgiveness of your sins. And you will receive the gift of the Holy Spirit. The promise is for you and your children and for all who are far off—for all whom the Lord our God will call."

With many other words he warned them; and he pleaded with them, "Save yourselves from this corrupt generation." Those who accepted his message were baptized, and about three thousand were added to their number that day. (Acts 2:36–41)

The miraculous events of this day and the powerful preaching of Peter had convinced many in the great Pentecost Day throng that they had sinned grievously in rejecting God's Messiah. Peter's answer gave them hope. They could repent, put their faith in Jesus, and show this new orientation by being baptized, with baptism *"in the name of Jesus Christ"* being *"for the forgiveness of [their] sins"* (2:38).

The fact that baptism is done in the "name of Jesus" reminds us of the point we made at the beginning of the book: *Baptism means nothing apart from Jesus.* What caused baptism to bring the forgiveness of sins was not the act itself, or God forbid, something in the water, but the fact that it was done "in the name of Jesus the Messiah," which indicated the person involved was coming to Jesus, putting trust in Jesus, and looking to Jesus for forgiveness. In a word, what brought forgiveness of sins was *Jesus*.

Yet, there would have been no controversy on that day about the exact time one was forgiven—as in, was it when you just believed, or was it when you repented, or only after you believed, repented and were baptized? There would simply have been celebration that God's grace was available and that one could receive it by turning away from an old life and turning to Jesus and obeying the good news by submitting to a Jesus baptism. No one there that day who witnessed that scene where three thousand were baptized would have questioned if there was any connection between baptism *in Jesus' name* and salvation and forgiveness of sins.

The tortured type of exegesis that would conclude that only repentance, and not baptism, was linked with forgiveness or that baptism was done only because one's sins were *already* forgiven would not come for another seventeen or eighteen hundred years when many were committed to reading every text through a dogma of "faith alone."

In the Book of Acts we have many more stories of conversions to Jesus, with almost all of them including references to their baptisms. We have actually three reports of

Saul's conversion—two of those being reported in Saul's (or Paul's) own words. The clearer of those two is found in Acts 22 where he describes his shocking encounter with Jesus on the Damascus road, how that led to temporary blindness, and then how a man came to him. Here is Paul's account of what happened next, as told by Luke:

> "He stood beside me and said, 'Brother Saul, receive your sight!' And at that very moment I was able to see him. Then he said: 'The God of our fathers has chosen you to know his will and to see the Righteous One and to hear words from his mouth. You will be his witness to all men of what you have seen and heard. And now what are you waiting for? Get up, be baptized and wash your sins away, calling on his name.'" (Acts 22:13–16)

Paul had three days in darkness to contemplate his op-position to God's long-awaited Messiah. His mind had surely gone over and over the events of recent months, and he understood, as he would later write, that he was "a blas-phemer and a persecutor and a violent man" (1 Timothy 1:13), nothing less than the chief of sinners (1:15 KJV). Now a man has come, given him back his sight, and told him God has plans for him. But, maybe best of all, he told him that his sins can be washed away.

### Baptism: The Real 'Sinner's Prayer'

The message is like the one in Acts 2. It *was* a message about a sinner's prayer—only not the one taught so often in our day. Saul was to *call on the name of the Lord*—the Righteous One he had seen and heard, but he was to do it in baptism where his sins would be washed away. Could it be that this language (which occurs only here), though true for us all, was especially for Saul? Surely he was feeling the weight of enormous guilt and needing an image of something great enough to carry it all way. And so like powerful floods remove foundations from houses and wash them away, Paul is assured that his sin can be mightily removed. The same assurance comes to us in our day.

But once again, what is the key? "Calling on his name." Sin is not washed away by baptism unless baptism is focused on Jesus and submitted to with a heart that is calling on him. But when that heart is there and baptism is done in his name, calling on him, it brings a flood of grace and forgiveness that carries our sin far away. Baptism is the occasion of our forgiveness, but only because it is the God-appointed place to call on Jesus' name—confessing him as both our Lord and our Savior.

In an unusual passage in 1 Peter 3, the apostle who first called people to be baptized in the name of Jesus for the forgiveness of their sins described baptism in prayer-like terms when he wrote of its connection to salvation. We have to pay careful attention to get his point, and not get side-tracked by a difficult phrase or two:

> For Christ also suffered for sins once for all, the righteous for the unrighteous, in order to bring you to God. He was put to death in the flesh, but made alive in the spirit, in which also he went and made a proclamation to the spirits in prison, who in former times did not obey, when God waited patiently in the days of Noah, during the building of the ark, in which a few, that is, eight persons, were saved through water. And baptism, which this prefigured, now saves you—not as a removal of dirt from the body, but as an appeal to God for a good conscience, through the resurrection of Jesus Christ. (1 Peter 3:18–21 NRSV)

It is beyond our present purpose to explore all the elements in this fascinating and difficult text, but in Peter's thinking there is a parallel between the water in the days of Noah and Christian baptism. Here are three different translations of the key phrase in v21:

- "And this water symbolizes baptism that now saves you." (NIV)

- "And this prefigured baptism, which now saves you." (NET)

- "Corresponding to that, baptism now saves you." (NASB)

We naturally think of the ark saving the eight souls in Noah's day, but in Peter's analogy the water "saved" because it separated the family from the old sinful world. In a similar way Christians have passed through the water of baptism and have been saved out of an old sinful life and brought into a new Kingdom. But Peter is quick to clarify what he means by saying that baptism "saves." It is not because the physical act removes something outward. No, it saves for two reasons.

First, baptism is the appeal to God for a clear conscience. In this sense it is correct to call baptism "the sinner's prayer." As in Paul's case, it is where we call on the name of the Lord and acknowledge our need.

Second, baptism derives all its power from Jesus, and in this case, Peter says from "the resurrection of Jesus Christ." It would have not been surprising if he had said from "the cross of Jesus Christ," but in New Testament thinking, the two always go together. With the use of synecdoche, to speak of one is to include the other. The bottom line of this passage in 1 Peter is that baptism does bring deliverance (it saves) but not because it is something "good" that we do. Rather, it is an appeal to Jesus who through the power of his resurrection is able to save those in need.

## *Living the Baptized Life*

As we try to appreciate what it means to live the baptized life, let's return to Saul (soon to be Paul) and his experience. Days before Ananias came to him, he had been lying on the ground, blinded by the dazzling light and asking, "Who are you, Lord?" and hearing what must have been, at least in that moment, a terrifying answer. "I am Jesus, whom you are persecuting...."

For weeks, at least, or maybe more, Saul had been pouring all his energy into opposing the burgeoning Jesus movement. Now it was clear that all his righteousness was indeed as filthy rags. "I am Jesus, whom you are persecuting." But surely he later would have agreed with the words of the great spiritual inspired by his story: "Happy day, Oh happy day, when Jesus washed my sins away."

As we have seen, a spirit of confession is one that must always accompany baptism. We are recognizing our own sin and need, confessing that need, and appealing to Jesus for his cleansing and forgiveness. Therefore, the baptized life will be characterized by an ongoing spirit of confession. Self-righteousness has no place here. We must continue to humble ourselves before God and before others, just as we did in baptism.

It is easy to believe that for the rest of his life Paul would, again and again, see himself rising out of baptism knowing that through Jesus his foolishness, self-righteousness and vitriol were all washed away.

With that in mind, no wonder he would write, "Be kind and compassionate to one another, forgiving each other, just as in Christ God forgave you" (Ephesians 4:32) and "Bear with each other and forgive whatever grievances you may have against one another. Forgive as the Lord forgave you" (Colossians 3:13). To live out one's baptism is to marvel at one's forgiveness and to be so willing to forgive others.

## Pay It Forward

In the wake of the terrible school shooting in Newtown, Connecticut, in December 2012, newswoman Ann Curry began a campaign on social media to encourage people to commit to twenty-six acts of kindness in honor of the twenty-six victims in the school. For weeks people wrote in to tell about how they were doing such things as paying the toll for the person in line behind them or paying the bill for someone in a restaurant. The phrase "pay it forward," made popular by a movie some years ago, came back into vogue. All kinds of people found themselves being the benefactors of someone's kindness, creating the desire to pay it forward to someone else.

In a similar way, but in a much greater sense, the baptized life is the life of paying it forward. It is extending to others the same kind of kindness and generosity and for-giveness that God through Jesus has extended to us. I find that many disciples struggle mightily with Jesus' kingdom teaching for us to love our enemies. But would we struggle so much if we kept in mind Paul's words:

> For if, when we were God's enemies, we were rec-onciled to him through the death of his Son, how much more, having been reconciled, shall we be saved through his life? (Romans 5:10)

We should be most thankful that God is absolutely committed to the teaching on loving enemies. Otherwise, we would still be in our sin. For when we were his ene-mies, he loved and offered costly forgiveness to us.

I wrote parts of this chapter a week after a horrendous terrorist attack in Boston—a place I called home for eight-een years. Events unfolded there on streets I had traveled many times.

I read in the *Boston Globe* that on Sunday a minister stood before a famous congregation in that city and preached the message of forgiveness and called on all to have a heart to forgive the perpetrators, who were known by this time, even as they comforted the victims. News re-ports said the audience was completely silent. That may have been because that audience is always silent, but I have a feeling it was more silent than ever. One would hope that in some of our more demonstrative churches, and churches committed to the kingdom message, words such as these would have been met with a chorus of "Amens."

Within four days of the attack the two bombing suspects were located, and one was killed in a gun battle with police. Now as I write, no cemetery has been willing to allow the dead man to be buried therein. Town after town refused to accept the body.

People do not live lives overflowing with forgiveness. Emotionally it is sometimes hard to get there, but living the baptized life means remembering how much we have all been forgiven and paying it forward—yes, to people just as undeserving as we are. Yes, even to our enemies and those who do us harm. Yes, to all those "other" people.

Many believers, after baptism, describe the feeling of having a heavy weight lifted off them. Sin and guilt are heavy to bear. Having God take it all away is amazing and should lead to some amazingly gracious interactions with others when we live as men and women who have poverty of spirit but deeply appreciate our forgiveness and salvation.

*For this reason let everyone esteem his Baptism as a daily dress in which he is to walk constantly...*

## Questions for
## Study and Discussion

1. Why might some think that baptism is a work that is needed to complete one's salvation?

2. What is the significance of the passive voice in the baptismal passages referenced in this chapter?

3. On a continuum, have you been more on the side that baptism is something we do or that what happens in baptism is what God does? If a correction is needed, how would you make an adjustment?

4. In what sense is baptism "the biblical sinner's prayer"?

5. Why should we be very concerned about replacing something biblical with another idea of our own?

6. Understanding the connection between baptism and salvation, what is most challenging to you about living the baptized life?

# 5

# BAPTISM
# AND
# CHRIST'S DEATH

One of the most remarkable facts concerning the Christian faith is that it spread rapidly in a hostile and calloused world even though at the heart of the message was a symbol universally seen as repulsive. We are talking, of course, about the cross.

> Crucifixion was invented by the Persians and perfected by the Romans as a means of discouraging rebels and runaway slaves. It produced horrifying effects on its victims that have seldom been equaled. The suffering of Jesus was so great that it was four centuries before any Christian dared to portray it in art. From the earliest days of the Christian movement, Christians created art forms to show everything from the descending of the Holy Spirit at Jesus' baptism to the Last Supper. But not one crucifixion

scene can be found until the fifth century, a hundred
years after the Romans had ended the practice and
at a time when no one was around with firsthand
knowledge of its horrors.[1]

It is hard for us in the twenty-first century to find anything that we can compare to crucifixion. Torture, of
course, is not unknown in our day, but we, thankfully, hear
of few things designed to bring about such a public, humiliating, slow and agonizing death. But what is rare in
our world was common in biblical times. There would
have been few Jews living in Palestine at the time of Jesus
who had never seen someone crucified. Jesus was neither
the first nor the last to have died this awful death. The Romans used crucifixion to powerfully control society.

### Take Up Your Crosses

When Jesus taught "If anyone would come after me,
he must deny himself and take up his cross daily and follow me" (Luke 9:23), his listeners didn't know all that
meant, but they surely understood the call much better
than we do. His closest followers would have been shaken
by his words that he was going to suffer and die, but now
he was letting them know that being his follower would
also mean a cross for them. Was this all madness? "He who
fears he shall suffer already suffers what he fears," wrote

---

1. Thomas Cahill, *Desire of the Everlasting Hills: The World Before and After
Jesus* (New York: Nan A. Talese, 1999), 285.

Michel de Montaigne. They certainly must have feared what they would suffer, and they must have suffered what they feared. It is little wonder that after this word from Jesus, he took his inner circle with him to the Mount of Transfiguration to see his glory and hear God say, "This is my Son whom I have chosen; listen to him" (Luke 9:35). They were in need of some confirmation and reassurance.

Matthew and Mark both describe Peter's reaction to Jesus' earlier statement about his soon-to-come suffering and death (Matthew 16:22, Mark 8:32). Peter's rebuke of Jesus led to a conversation that ended with these famous words from Jesus: "Get behind me, Satan. You don't have in mind the things of God, but the things of men" (Matthew 16:23, Mark 8:33).

Here we see clearly a theme found other places in Scripture: We can either approach life with God's wisdom or with human wisdom, but they go in different directions and have far different outcomes. The call to take up the cross looks like madness and folly. A decision to protect, guard and defend your life looks eminently more sensible. But Jesus goes on to say, "For whoever wants to save his life will lose it, but whoever loses his life for me will save it" (Luke 9:24). In God's economy the seed that falls into the ground and dies is the one that produces much fruit (John 12:24–25).

We would hardly be human if we didn't struggle with this teaching of Jesus, just as Peter and the other apostles did. Losing your life and dying to self, after all, is about as counterintuitive as it gets. I have Christian brothers and sisters who tell me that "self-preservation" and "self-defense" are most appropriate because God has made us this way.

We should be encouraged that the one who protested the loudest—our friend, Peter—eventually became one of the strongest advocates of what may be called "the way of the cross." Our natural resistance can be overcome. Writing in his first letter, he says:

> To this you were called, because Christ suffered for you, leaving you an example, that you should follow in his steps.

> "He committed no sin,
>     and no deceit was found in his mouth."

> When they hurled their insults at him, he did not retaliate; when he suffered, he made no threats. Instead, he entrusted himself to him who judges justly. He himself bore our sins in his body on the tree, so that we might die to sins and live for righteousness; by his wounds you have been healed. (1 Peter 2:21–24)

In this context, Peter calls on disciples to love one another deeply from the heart, rid themselves of all malice and deceit, hypocrisy, envy and slander of every kind, show proper respect to everyone, love the brotherhood of believers, fear God, and honor the king. Slaves were to submit to their masters, wives to their husbands, and husbands were to be men of prayer who were attuned to the needs of their wives. To live like this was to follow in Jesus' steps and go the way of the cross.

### The Cross Converges with Baptism

While all of the early Christian leaders are united in calling everyone to be a follower of Jesus who goes to the cross, it is Paul who most fully shows us how this teaching converges with baptism. Paul is often referred to as a "task theologian." Along with the writer of Hebrews, Paul wrote some of the deeper theological sections of the New Testament, but they almost always grew out of some need that had to be addressed—thus a "task" for him as a leader.

In Romans 5 we find him describing the peace we have with God because of the grace in which we stand. Paul even makes the point that where sin increased, grace increased all the more. However, whenever grace is preached, there is always the danger that it may be abused. But, then, any great teaching can be distorted.

And so, as we pointed out in chapter 1, it is here that Paul asks, "What shall we say, then? Shall we go on sinning so that grace may increase?" (6:1). If grace is not to be outdone, why not sin a great deal so that God's glorious grace will have occasion to just flood in and overcome it all the more?

That may seem like a logical question, and perhaps we should say, we are glad that it was asked because of what we learn from it. However, in the short run, it almost sends Paul off the ledge. Look at different translations of verse 2a:

- By no means! (NIV)
- Of course not! (NLT)
- May it never be! (NASB)
- God forbid. (KJV)
- Absolutely not! (HCSB)
- That's unthinkable! (GW)

By no means shall we go on sinning because "we died to sin; how can we live in it any longer?" (v2b). Yes, grace increased enough to cover all our sin, but grace also brought us to a place and time where we died to sin, where we made a decision to reject it, where we denied it and disowned it because it is so opposed to God. And where was that place and time? He takes them back to an experience that they had in common: baptism.

> Or don't you know that all of us who were baptized
> into Christ Jesus were baptized into his death? We
> were therefore buried with him through baptism
> into death in order that, just as Christ was raised

> from the dead through the glory of the Father, we
> too may live a new life. If we have been united with
> him like this in his death, we will certainly also be
> united with him in his resurrection. For we know
> that our old self was crucified with him so that the
> body of sin might be done away with, that we should
> no longer be slaves to sin. (Romans 6:3–6)

It is important for us to pay close attention to several phrases, each having great meaning. Read them slowly:

- "we died to sin"
- "baptized into Christ Jesus"
- "baptized into his death"
- "buried with him through baptism into death"
- "we, too [like him], may live a new life"
- "united with him like this in his death"
- "united with him in his resurrection"
- "old self was crucified with him"

Shall we sin more because God's grace is so abundant? Absolutely not! God forbid! May it never be! Because something life-changing has happened to us. In baptism we died to sin, we were immersed into Christ, went spiritually right into his death, shared his burial, had our old self laid in his tomb. We were united in his death and then were raised up to live a new life, united in his resurrection.

With the question of continuing in sin on the table, Paul goes to the place where everything changed for them. In baptism it all came together. There they admitted their need, there they confessed "Jesus is Lord," and there they came "into" him, were united with him, and were united with his death, burial and resurrection. If that sounds like baptism was viewed as dying to an old life and beginning a new life, I think we are getting it.

### Something Really Happens in Baptism

If your training or background has taught you to say that baptism is important, but it only *symbolizes* what has already happened to you or that it is just something you do as a testimony, I would appeal to you to read the text again to see if there is any indication of this understanding. As Robert Webber puts it, "Baptism says what it does and does what it says."[2]

Baptism is an outward sign of something inward, but it doesn't just symbolize something; it is where something really happens. This is the truth that Paul is reinforcing with these Christians. And, so, we can look back on our baptism and find that something happened there that needs to affect who we are and how we are today.

We need not be troubled that something spiritual is tied to something physical. That is the whole nature of the incarnation. God became flesh. As Robert Kolb, one of the contributors to *Understanding Four Views of Baptism,* rightly

---

2. Webber, *The Divine Embrace,* 155.

observes, "God is at home in his creation, and he selects elements from the material created order, like human language, as well as human flesh and blood, to carry out his saving will."[3]

It is a Greek view, not a biblical view, which demands that spiritual experiences be purely inward only involving the spirit and not the body, or only the spiritual and not the physical. This was a primary reason the Gnostic teachers, according to Tertullian, wanted to "destroy baptism," and even more heretically, wanted to destroy the incarnation and have a Christ who did not take on flesh.[4] Unwittingly, those who want to separate baptism from new birth can make the same serious mistake.

### *Participate in Jesus' Death*

But our main point here is that Paul says in baptism we participate in Jesus' death. From there we will go on to share in the resurrection (to be discussed in the next chapter).

Certainly, there is more to taking up the cross than being baptized, but in baptism we are agreeing with God's verdict that our old self needs to die and the rest of our lives will need to be a reaffirmation of that death. Look again at Paul's words:

- "we died to sin"

- "baptized into his death"

---

3. Robert Kolb, contributor, *Understanding Four Views of Baptism*, series ed., Paul Ingle (Grand Rapids: Zondervan, 2007), 48.

4. "On Baptism," *Ante-Nicene Fathers, vol. 3*, page 669.

- "buried with him through baptism into death"
- "old self was crucified with him"

All these phrases are so in line with Jesus' call for us to deny ourselves, take up the cross and follow him. I suspect some will wonder why I did not include in this book a chapter on baptism and repentance since the two are so closely linked in Acts 2. That is likely a worthy idea, but I felt this chapter addresses the matter of repentance. Prior to Jesus, all of us were living a life shaped by the world's wisdom that essentially says, "You're better off putting yourself at the center of your life."

I read these words recently from a popular blogger that sum up the world's wisdom quite well: "You are the light. Your inner purpose is to connect with that light." Repentance involves a turning away from that kind of thinking. It says, "I am not the light, I am not the answer, I don't have the answers, and living by myself and for myself is not God's plan." Repentance means we say, "I am ready to die to my confidence in me, and I am ready to follow Jesus with confidence in him."

Baptism is such a vivid picture of that decision. Years ago my wife, Sheila, was invited to a women's meeting in another church. The speaker urged the women to make a decision to follow Jesus and pray to "receive" him right there. Then, she encouraged those who made that decision to go home and do something to show that this was a decisive moment, something that would help them remember it. She suggested something like going into the backyard and driving a nail into a tree.

That reminds me of Robert Webber's challenge to his evangelical friends not to create substitutes for baptism, such as walking an aisle in a "crusade" or raising your hand.[5] Which do we want—a sign or identifying mark from men or one that comes from heaven? Why drive a nail into a tree when God has given us baptism?

Our burial in water so clearly shows what we are doing—dying and putting an old life away. And that happens because we are coming to be baptized *into Christ*. If Christ were not there to meet us, nothing would happen. If we were not being united in his death, our old ways would not be dealt with. We cannot determinedly end our old lives. Whatever we do with our strong-willed determination is just more of the old us. We can only end an old life by yielding to Christ and finding union with him. The picture I have of baptism is me coming before the judge who says, "Do you have anything to say for yourself?" I respond, "No, judge, there is nothing good in me, that is in my sinful nature. I disown (deny) my 'self.' I just need to be put to death." As I yield to Jesus, he does what I cannot do. He puts my old life to death and he raises me up to a

---

5. Webber, *The Divine Embrace*, 153.

new life. All the credit goes to him because it is all his work.

In a similar passage in Colossians Paul enlarges on what happens in baptism.

> In him you were also circumcised, in the putting off of the sinful nature, not with a circumcision done by the hands of men but with the circumcision done by Christ, having been buried with him in baptism and raised with him through your faith in the power of God, who raised him from the dead. When you were dead in your sins and in the uncircumcision of your sinful nature, God made you alive with Christ. He forgave us all our sins. (Colossians 2:11–13)

We see Paul describing a circumcision unlike that known in Judaism, for this involves the spiritual removal of the sinful nature *and it is done by Christ.* But it is evident that spiritual circumcision is conjoined to baptism by the use of a participial phrase, "having been buried with him in baptism," that modifies the previous verb regarding the "putting off" of the sinful nature. We are circumcised spiritually as we are buried with Christ in baptism.

This is reinforced in the statement in verse 13: "When you were dead in your sins and in the uncircumcision of your sinful nature, God made you alive with Christ. He forgave us all our sins."

Later in verse 20 Paul builds on this idea: "Since you died with Christ to the basic principles of this world, why, as though you still belonged to it, do you submit to its rules?" He is basically saying, since your old life was cut away when you were buried with Christ in baptism, and since you left your old life there with its adherence to the principles of this world, why are you still following those principles (in this case ascetic practices of spirituality or just more rules made by men)? The idea of "you died" is prominent here but even more so in the next section in chapter 3.

> Since, then, you have been raised with Christ, set your hearts on things above, where Christ is seated at the right hand of God. Set your minds on things above, not on earthly things. For you died, and your life is now hidden with Christ in God. When Christ, who is your life, appears, then you also will appear with him in glory. (Colossians 3:1–4)

With these events—(1) circumcision of the sinful nature, (2) burial with Christ in baptism, and (3) resurrection through faith—in mind from the previous chapter, Paul appeals to them to live a life that takes direction from above and not from the earth. Give it different names, but this is the circumcised life, the baptized life and the resurrected life.

This Colossians text is a great statement to make to someone as they emerge from the water of baptism. Who knows but that it was used this way in the early church? For the purposes of this chapter we want to emphasize verse 3: "For you died, and your life is now hidden with Christ in God." For a brief moment as we are immersed in the water, our bodies are hidden from view. We emerge having taken on a new identity. Our old lives are buried with Christ—hidden away—and our new lives are not about ourselves but about Christ. As Paul said in Galatians, "I have been crucified with Christ and I no longer live, but Christ lives in me. The life I live in the body, I live by faith in the Son of God, who loved me and gave himself for me" (2:20).

In Colossians 3 Paul goes on to spell out in very specific terms how a whole host of attitudes and qualities have to die because "you died." They include the following:

| | | |
|---|---|---|
| sexual immorality | greed | slander |
| impurity | anger | filthy language |
| lust | rage | racism |
| evil desires | malice | |

No list like this in the New Testament is ever complete, but we get the idea. At the heart of all these are two deadly qualities that must die: (1) pride and (2) selfishness.

One of the striking features of baptism certainly helps us deal with pride. In being baptized you put yourself (usually without any fashionable clothes on!) in the hands of another person or persons. You allow them to immerse you so that you come up as wet as a newborn baby. It is hard in such a moment to appear or even be prideful.

I have sometimes thought that it might be good, as we share life together in the body, if we had a collage of pictures showing all of us coming up out of the water from our baptisms. Or what if our church directories were composed of such pictures? There we would be seen as humble, joyful, unimpressive and childlike. Such a mental picture makes me laugh. Even envisioning such a thing is a great reminder that if the baptized life is to be anything, it is to be a life where pride has died and humility reigns.

And, of course, the ultimate expression of the kingdom life is that the old self-oriented self has been put to death, so that love can now flow freely. Paul goes on in Colossians 3 to say that out of that burial in baptism we should come forth to put on new garments such as compassion, kindness, humility, gentleness, and over everything else—love, which he says binds them all together (vv12–14). Baptism reminds us not just what we have died to, but what we have risen up to embrace.

In his book, *Reborn on the Fourth of July—The Challenge of Faith, Patriotism and Conscience,* Iraq War veteran Logan

Mehl–Laituri describes his baptism that took place on the Fourth of July 2006. Logan, an army sergeant at the time, articulately expresses what he understood it to mean for him:

> My baptism would be the first day of the rest of that life—a new life lived sacrificially, but a deeper sacrifice than when I donned the uniform of a soldier. If I was to take up my cross, it meant I would have to lay down my sword. Like Cain, I had a second chance to master the sin that crouches constantly at my door; I could reject the path of retribution and embrace the hard, redemptive way of Jesus. But in being baptized I was articulating that intent publicly so that I could be aided in my effort and held accountable when I failed.

> I never thought explicitly about taking my own life [like so many soldiers], but it is clear to me that I didn't have a sincere interest to live. In the midst of suicide bombers and terrorism, as I was thinking about what it meant to be a Christian, with its long history of martyrdom, I struggled to understand the difference between a suicide bomber and a Christian martyr. The language of baptism, after all, is laden with words about death. Being "reborn" assumes that one is rising from death. Death, it seems, is requisite to new life. But in adopting this mantle of new life, Christians recognize that their life is no longer theirs, but belongs to God. Our lives are living sacrifices;

not our own will, but God's, be done (Luke 22:42). We let it be with us according to God's desire (Luke 1:38). My movement toward baptism was not unlike my preparation for deployment; I was embracing death in each, but in very different ways.[6]

Logan understood that in dying with Christ we acknowledge that our life is no longer our own, but it belongs to God, and in baptism we are embracing a death in order that we might find real life. We will allow Logan to share his thoughts about his new resurrected life in the next chapter.

As I was writing this book, news came of the death of Christian scholar and philosopher Dallas Willard. One who knew him well said his books basically told us: "Come on over. It's going to be okay to die first. You have to do it, and you can do it. Not even Jesus got a resurrection without a death, and he'll be at your side when you surrender your old life. Trust me on this. If you die with Jesus Christ, God will walk you out of your tomb into a life of incomparable joy and purpose inside his boundless and competent love."

In *The Cost of Discipleship*, Dietrich Bonhoeffer famously wrote, "When Jesus calls a man, he bids him to come and die."[7] He completed that thought later in the

6. Logan Mehl–Laituri, *Reborn on the Fourth of July—The Challenge of Faith, Patriotism and Conscience* (Downers Grove, IL: IVP Books, 2012), Kindle location 1255.

7. Dietrich Bonhoeffer, *The Cost of Discipleship* (New York City: MacMillan, 1961), 89.

book when he wrote, "The cross of Christ is the death we undergo once and for all in our baptism and is a death full of grace."[8] In baptism, we die with Christ to an old life.

To live a baptized life, then, is to "take up [your] cross daily" (Luke 9:23), to "count yourselves dead to sin" (Romans 6:11), "to put off your old self" (Ephesians 4:23), and to "put to death, therefore, whatever belongs to your earthly nature" (Colossians 3:5). It is to die to self in your family, on the job, in your school and in your relationships. It is to lay down your life for the church even as Jesus did that very thing (Ephesians 5:25). It is to continue to affirm that the way to find your life is to lose it (Luke 9:24), and, then, to offer yourself as a living sacrifice (Romans 12:1) and to do that every new day.

*We, who have died to sin—how could we live in sin a moment longer? Have you forgotten that all of us who were baptized into Jesus Christ were, by that very action, sharing in his death? (Romans 6:3 Phillips)*

---

8. Bonhoeffer, *The Cost of Discipleship*, 232.

## Questions for Study and Discussion

1. How does the image of being baptized into Christ's death help us see that the disciple's life involves much more than feeling forgiven?

2. How do these thoughts about being baptized into Christ's death relate to repentance and baptism?

3. What are some of the things that we must remind ourselves that we left in the water when we were buried with Christ? Which of these are more of a challenge for you?

4. What elements of Logan's description of his baptism do you connect with?

5. Do you have a picture of yourself taken in or right after your baptism? Why are you likely not going to put that picture with your resume even if applying for a position with the church? But what is good about what that picture represents?

6. What is the connection between dying with Christ and living a life of love? Why is that life of love the ultimate mark of the baptized life?

# 6

# BAPTISM AND RESURRECTION

In preaching the Gospel of the Kingdom, Jesus was saying that the end of history was breaking into our present age. The age to come was dawning. On the face of it, that sounds like something powerful, and, fittingly, Jesus said to his disciples,

> "I tell you the truth, some who are standing here will not taste death before they see the kingdom of God come with power." (Mark 9:1)

The writer of Hebrews was confident that those who had become Christians had "tasted...the powers of the coming age" (Hebrews 6:5). The message of the Kingdom is about something powerful that has happened and continues to happen.

## The Kingdom Shakes Things Up

From time to time we see a headline about how close an asteroid will come to our earth. As I was writing this chapter, a meteor rained down on a city in Siberia injuring over 1000 people with its sonic boom.

Coincidentally, that same day an asteroid came about as close to earth as one has in many years. Scientists tell us that in the history of earth, asteroids have actually broken through the earth's atmosphere and crashed into our planet in a disruptive way.

If a large asteroid struck earth today, it could create a dust storm that would plunge the planet into a nuclear winter. Were it to land in the ocean, it could set off a cataclysmic tsunami that would have worldwide impact. Such ideas are the stuff of Hollywood productions.

However, before you put this possibility on a list of things to worry about, consider that scientists estimate that cataclysmic events like these occur only about once every 1000 centuries.

But here's the point: If something in our universe came crashing in from outside our nice operating system on earth, its power would be felt. It would shake things up.

In the same way, if the Kingdom of God did come crashing into first century Palestine in the life and person of Jesus, we would expect that power would be felt. Maybe not in the same physical way as an asteroid's impact, but a power, nonetheless, that produces some remarkable spiritual impact.

And this is exactly the story the New Testament tells us. All four Gospels affirm that the resurrection of Jesus from the dead took place and that this event became the driving force for a movement that spread across a vast, mighty *and hostile* empire (and beyond) in less than a century.

### No Human Sense

We must consider the reasons why such a messianic movement made no human sense and should never have happened.

1. The Jewish expectation was a victorious Messiah who would marshal the forces of God and militarily expel the foreign invaders from the land of promise. Jesus completely failed the test.

2. One of the chief symbols of Roman dominance was the cross. Through the use of this tortuous form of death, Rome was able to strike fear into the hearts of those contemplating rebellion.

3. The Roman crucifixion of Jesus would have meant that the hopes of Jesus' disciples were devastated. A worse outcome could not have been imagined. There was nothing about this event that would have caused them to take heart.

4. The crucifixion would have convinced curious Jews on the margins that Jesus was indeed another imposter or false messiah. Disciples, and those who were not, would have recalled Deuteronomy 21:23: "…anyone who is hung on a pole is under God's curse." Disciples would have said, well…what they actually did say was, "We had hoped he was the one who was going to redeem Israel" (Luke 24:21).

5. While crucifixion was an abomination to Jews, it was the picture of utter foolishness and failure to Romans and Greeks. It was the death of slaves and that of conquered and humiliated people. Can you imagine what late night comics (for whom nothing is sacred) and *Saturday Night Live* would have done with the story of a crucified lord and savior?

And yet, within a few years across the Roman Empire, astoundingly, this crucified Jewish man was worshipped as a god by Jews and Gentiles. Indeed he was worshipped as *the* Lord and *the* God! Can you stop a moment and let this soak in? What caused such a radical change? What could possibly have transformed a Roman cross into something that the disciples would say demonstrated the power of God?

I like Mike Erre's words: This was a movement that would "triumph not by inflicting violence but by enduring it—not by coercing or humiliating others but by enduring humiliation with gentle dignity."[1] But what caused such a movement?

## Power of the Resurrection

The biblical explanation is that the Kingdom came with power. Like an asteroid, it came breaking into their world—not crushing believers but empowering them. Those men and women who had surely been in despair, depression or dismay were energized and emboldened. "With great power the apostles continued to testify to the resurrection of the Lord Jesus, and much grace was upon them all" (Acts 4:33).

The resurrection that many Jews were sure would come to the nation *at the end of history* occurred in one man *right in the middle of history.* Those who, by almost all earthly metrics, were powerless experienced a power from way beyond themselves. And, so, this upside-down message went out from Jerusalem and all the way to Rome and beyond.

Repeatedly the New Testament writers speak of the power of the resurrection—this victory over death and this appearance of a new order of life—brought to those who receive the Kingdom of God.

- Jesus is the one "who through the Spirit of holiness was declared with power to be the Son of God by his resurrection from the dead" (Romans 1:4).

1. Mike Erre, *Death by Church* (Eugene, OR: Harvest House, 209), 150.

- Paul longs to "know Christ and the power of his resurrection and the fellowship of sharing in his sufferings, becoming like him in his death" (Philippians 3:10).

- Peter praises God that "he has given us new birth into a living hope through the resurrection of Jesus Christ from the dead" and then adds that this means we "through faith are shielded by God's power until the coming of the salvation that is ready to be revealed in the last time" (1 Peter 1:3, 5).

- Paul shows the implication for believers when he writes, "By his power God raised the Lord from the dead, and he will raise us also" (1 Corinthians 6:14).

- The same writer reaches into his bag of adjectives in writing Ephesians to speak of God's "incomparably great power for us who believe." Then he adds, "That power is like the working of his mighty strength, which he exerted in Christ when he raised him from the dead and seated him at his right hand in the heavenly realms" (Ephesians 1:19–20).

## More Than a Doctrine to Be Believed

It is sometimes said that the resurrection is one of the essential doctrines of the church. Paul is certainly saying this in his lengthy treatment of the resurrection in 1 Corinthians 15. But what must be seen is that the resurrection is far more than a doctrine to be believed.

We often ask a person about to be baptized if they believe Jesus died and rose again. This is well and good, but there is more. The person also needs confidence that through Jesus and by his power, they, too, can die and be raised right in the middle of this present age.

The resurrection is spoken of in two ways in Scripture. On the one hand, it is a very real event in history, like the Jewish Exodus, which is to be believed and cherished. But on the other hand, it is also a reality with which the believer can and must intersect and connect. The disciple's relationship to the resurrection is not well represented in figure A.

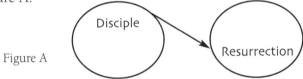

Figure A

It is not just an event in history to observe and study and write about. It is not just something to believe to be true. This is useful, but it is not kingdom living. What the New Testament describes is something that is much better, shown by figure B (though no illustration is perfect).

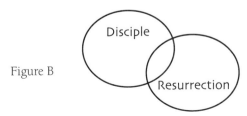

Figure B

Here we see there is an intersection between the resurrection and the disciple. The person does not just believe it to be true, like an observer might have believed Jesus fed the multitude. The disciple *participates* in the resurrection, and in some very real sense becomes united with the resurrection so that the new life that characterizes resurrection life makes its way into their experience.

### Intersection Takes Place in Baptism

We must go again, this time with a different focus, to the language of Romans 6 which emphasizes our participation in the resurrection, as well as something else that is significant:

> What shall we say, then? Shall we go on sinning so that grace may increase? By no means! We died to sin; how can we live in it any longer? Or don't you know that all of us who were baptized into Christ Jesus were baptized into his death? We were therefore buried with him through baptism into death in order that, *just as Christ was raised* from the dead through the glory of the Father, *we too may live a new life.*
>
> If we have been united with him like this in his death, we will certainly also be *united with him in his resurrection.* For we know that our old self was crucified with him so that the body of sin might be

done away with, that we should no longer be slaves
to sin—because anyone who has died has been freed
from sin. Now if we died with Christ, we believe that
we will also live with him. (Romans 6:1–8, emphasis
added)

The passage shows not only that the disciple is united
with the resurrection of Christ, but it clearly describes
where this intersection takes place, and it is in baptism. As
we saw in the last chapter, baptism was being "baptized
into his death." It was having "our old self crucified with
him." It was being "buried with him." But then just as we
are "united with him like this in his death" we also share
in his resurrection. "Just as Christ was raised" so, too, we
are raised to "live a new life" in the here and now. We are
"united with him in his resurrection."

His point is that you come out of baptism "a raised
man," "a resurrected woman," "a new creation." An old life
has died with Jesus and a new person has been raised up
by the Holy Spirit (as Romans 8 will make clear). And so
the answer to the question Paul poses ("Shall we go on sinning so that grace may increase?") is another question:
"Why in the world would a new, resurrected person, enjoying the powers of the age to come, want to go back and
dabble in the very sin that stands opposed to this new life?"

It is this passage that gives us every reason to talk about

the "baptized life." Paul is saying to his readers, "Just live in view of your baptism. Remember what God did and what you became." You can almost hear Paul saying, "Just sit down and meditate on what took place in your baptism and now live consistently with this."

## Is Baptism Symbolic?

Was baptism in some way symbolic for Paul? I would say that if it were, it was also far more than that. Paul had command of several languages including Greek. Had he wanted to say that baptism merely symbolizes your resurrection with Christ, he could have easily done so, but he makes a much stronger statement.

Whatever we teach and practice regarding baptism, we should do it in a way that makes it possible for those we teach and mentor to identify completely with everything Paul says here. If our message causes people to conclude that their baptism was a good but peripheral matter (just something to take care of later), they will miss Paul's message. And, remembering the context of his remarks, they may very well go on sinning, thinking wrongly about grace, forgiveness and new life in Christ.

Every disciple needs to be able to read Romans 6 and say, "That is me" and "That describes what happened to me." They need to see their baptism just the way Paul describes it—the place and time when and where we are united with Christ in his death, his burial, and, praise God, his resurrection and his new life. *But even more than that, we need to see this as a call to a life to be lived now.* This is Paul's real point.

He is not encouraging nostalgia or the breaking into a few verses of "Precious Memories" (though I like that song, particularly the bluegrass renditions). He is not just reminding them of a sweet moment in their past. He is calling them to live as someone God made them to be in their baptism into Christ. Baptism, precisely because it is baptism *into Christ*, is all about new life…a life to be lived.

### Main Point of Romans 6

In the previous chapter, we saw the parallel between Romans 6 and a section in Colossians. Let's put the thoughts from Colossians together:

> …having been buried with him in baptism and raised with him through your faith in the power of God, who raised him from the dead. (2:12)

> Since, then, you have been raised with Christ, set your hearts on things above, where Christ is seated at the right hand of God. Set your minds on things above, not on earthly things. (3:1–2)

The result of baptism is resurrection to new life. Now since that has happened, one's mind should be set *on things above*, not on earthly things. This is reminiscent of the way Jesus taught us to pray: "Your kingdom come, your will be done, or earth *as it is in heaven*" (Matthew 6:10, emphasis added).

The age to come has broken into our lives in Jesus and the Spirit, changing us into resurrected people. Now we want the Kingdom to keep breaking in so we do God's will on earth as it is in heaven, living the future in the here and now. Our direction now comes from heaven as it also will be after the final resurrection and the consummation of the Kingdom.

Once again the words of Sergeant Logan Mehl–Laituri, from his book, *Reborn on the Fourth of July*, are a powerful illustration of this New Testament idea of being resurrected to live a new life:

> Harland prayed over me as he and Nathan each had one hand on my back and the other holding an arm; "God, please accept Logan as a follower of your Son, Jesus Christ." I looked at Nathan as he uttered those timeless words:
>
> "I baptize you in the name of the Father, the Son and the Holy Spirit."
>
> With that I was gently lowered backward into the water.... I felt like I was underwater forever, but it surely was only for a split second: eyes closed. I was

bathed in the warmth of the company of brothers in Christ. The radiance of the pool lamp breaking through my eyelids evoked the light of Jesus, illuminating our journey of faith.

I felt Nathan and Harlan urge me back to the surface, which rushed to meet me too soon. I wished I could stay in the pool forever. As I broke into the balmy Honolulu air, the water cascaded off my face and poured out my ears. I could hear the clapping of the crowd. As the final droplets fell from my eyes, the clapping mixed with the sound of a handful of fireworks set off long after the end of the official [Fourth of July] demonstration. They were baffling and beautiful in their timing; the heavens seemed to be rejoicing. My ears rang and my heart sang with each pyrotechnic burst.[2]

. . .

With fire and water, my baptism was sacramentally paralleling the failed rescue attempt in northern Iraq. There I had fought back the frigid scepter of death in the midst of the wilderness with my combat battle buddies. Here I found new and everlasting life bathed in the warm light of living water with a new band of brothers. Before I had been dragged from the dark waters, numb, cold and surrounded by death. Now I was being lifted by a new community, warm,

---

2. Mehl–Laituri, *Reborn*, Kindle location 1287.

alive and covered with light. The old things were being made new; life was bursting forth through, and despite, death.[3]

In his "exit interview" with his captain and commanding officer ten days after his baptism, Logan heard these words: "I don't believe you're a conscientious objector. I don't believe any of this religion...this conversion nonsense at all. I believe that you think you've hit on the perfect scheme to get out of the deployment because no one can prove you're not a conscientious objector.... Your conduct is not becoming of a non-commissioned officer.... You are not worthy of going to Iraq with us.... That's why the colonel and I made the decision to get rid of you as fast as we possibly can."[4]

Those are tough words. But Logan describes a different perspective he was able to hold on to after dying with Christ and being raised to a new life:

"Family" takes on a whole new meaning in baptism. If the army refused to acknowledge the truth about me, and I landed in jail because of conscientious objection, that would not change who I was. My identity is internally dictated; it comes from my heart where God has written a higher law.[5]

---

3. Mehl-Laituri, *Reborn,* Kindle location 1290.
4. Ibid, Kindle location 1374.
5. Ibid, Kindle Location 1382.

### Citizenship in Heaven

Paul's thinking is along the same lines as Logan's when he reminds the Philippians that "our citizenship is in heaven" (3:20). Philippian residents had long prided themselves on their Roman citizenship. But now disciples have died to old idolatries and old allegiances, and they have been raised to live in allegiance to what is above.

While writing this, I noticed a Twitter post from Rick Warren that read: "We make our commitments, then our commitments make us. Never give first class allegiance to second class causes." For the disciple, his first class allegiance is to the first class cause—the Kingdom of God. Being raised with Christ means the future has burst into the present, and we begin to live now what we will be in the future.

This lifestyle is the one we saw earlier described in Colossians 3, one characterized by compassion, kindness, humility, gentleness, patience, forgiveness and love (vv12–14). These qualities will not only be shown to others in the family of God but to the poor, the hurting and the lost of this world—including our enemies (Romans 12:20). This is a whole new world we are talking about, or at least the living out of a whole new world in the midst of an old one.

But how powerful will this resurrected life appear to be? Since it is based on the world above and the coming age, and since it is a life of servanthood and not a life of dominance, it may not impress those on earth. It did not impress Logan's commanding officer. It may look as weak as Jesus looked to Pilate, but because it is from above, it will quietly heal and transform what it touches.

So, shall we go on sinning that grace may increase? Absolutely not! What a ghastly thought! We have been rescued from the dominion of darkness, united with Christ in his resurrection, brought into the Kingdom of the Son he loves, and made to be citizens of heaven who live on earth seeking God's will and not our own. The kingdom life, the baptized life, the resurrected life—they are all the same.

*We were dead and buried with him in baptism, so that just as he was raised from the dead by that splendid Revelation of the Father's power so we too might rise to life on a new plane altogether. (Romans 6:4 Phillips)*

# Questions for
# Study and Discussion

1. How is Jesus' resurrection related to his teaching about the Kingdom of God?

2. What has convinced you that his resurrection was real?

3. What is the difference between believing the resurrection as a doctrine and experiencing it as a reality?

4. What strikes you about Logan's description of his baptism? How are some of his images helpful to you?

5. What role does the truth of Jesus' resurrection play in your own spiritual life?

# 7

# BAPTISM AND THE SPIRIT

The New Testament speaks of the Father, the Son and the Holy Spirit. To put it in the simplest of terms, the biblical teaching that God is our Father means that the Creator loves humankind. The teaching that Jesus is the Son means that God entered into our world to rescue and deliver us into a new way of living. The teaching about the Holy Spirit means that God is still at work in his world and particularly in his elect and chosen people, enabling them to live the new life.

We have said several times that baptism receives all its meaning from what God has done and is doing in Christ. This means we must also say that everything about baptism receives its meaning from the Holy Spirit, and that everything that happens in baptism happens as a result of the Spirit's work. In all we have talked about so far, the Holy Spirit has been at work. If the baptized life is not the Spirit-filled life, it is not a new life.

## *Enter the Holy Spirit*

The Holy Spirit enters early in our story. John the Baptizer taught that when the Messiah came there would be an immersion in the Holy Spirit. Jesus' earliest statement about entering the Kingdom was about a new birth or a birth from above that would be of the water *and the Spirit* (John 3:1–5). He described streams of living water that would flow out of those who believed in him, and John tells us that Jesus was speaking of the Holy Spirit that would be given after he had been glorified (John 7:38–39).

Jesus devoted much of his final upper room discourse to teaching about the coming of the *Paraclete*—the Encourager, the Counselor, the Comforter—who was the Holy Spirit (John 14–16). After Jesus' resurrection, he taught about the Kingdom of God for forty days, and then told his disciples to wait until they received power from the Holy Spirit (Acts 1:4, 8). Nothing was going to happen apart from the work of the Spirit.

In Acts 2 the Spirit comes upon the apostles on the day of Pentecost, fulfilling Joel 2. This pouring out of the Spirit immersed the apostles in the Spirit's power and was demonstrated in various ways—most notably in their ability to speak languages they had not learned and their ability to do miraculous healings.

With the Spirit's power Peter preached to a great crowd gathered on that special feast day and then concluded with the promise that all who turned to Jesus in repentance and were baptized would receive forgiveness and the gift of the Holy Spirit.

Without a doubt, Luke wanted us to know that what Peter preached was the normative message, for he tells us that Peter added: "This promise is for you and for your children [the next generation] and for all those who far off [the Gentiles], and as many as the Lord our God will call" (Acts 2:39).

When the gospel goes to Samaria carried by Philip, people are baptized in the name of Jesus, but we are told that they did not receive the Spirit until the apostles came and laid hands on them (Acts 8). With this anomaly, it appears the Spirit did not come to these believers immediately in order to make a point.

This absence brought some apostles to Samaria to connect with the Samaritans and lay hands on them for them to receive the Spirit. The promise was fulfilled, but just not immediately. The result of the circumstance was that the Samaritans were fully accepted as brothers and sisters, since no one could question that the apostles had affirmed them.

When the message goes for the first time to Gentiles in Acts 10, we have the opposite situation, and a more pronounced departure from the normative, as the Spirit comes on new believers *prior* to their baptism, in this case to make another point—namely to a hesitant and balking Peter—that the Gentiles were to be accepted. Seeing this, Peter exclaims, "Can anyone keep these people from being baptized with water? They have received the Holy Spirit just as we have" (Acts 10:47).

## Baptism and the Holy Spirit

There are some slight variations in the accounts through Acts 10, but one thing is consistent: Baptism and the coming of the Spirit are kept closely linked. This serves as a frequent reminder that the new life must be Spirit empowered.

Fairly complicated systems of theology have been developed to defend different views on the relationship of the Spirit to baptism as well as the actual work of the Spirit. Each view finds difficulty in harmonizing all of the texts with their teaching. Perhaps this is because the Spirit of God refuses to be placed in a box or to conform to a set of formulas (compare John 3:8).

I am aware of some rather complex and turbulent waters that we could try to navigate at this point, but it is beyond the scope of this book to exegete all the relevant passages needed for a thorough discussion of this topic. It is our purpose in this book to focus on what it means to live the baptized life. And with so many connections being made between baptism into Christ and the coming of the power of the Spirit, we want to stay faithful to our objective.

Wherever we land on some of these disputable matters, one thing must be seen as crystal clear, and we have already pointed it out: What John the Baptizer said about his baptism and that of Jesus and the Holy Spirit did not mean that baptism in water came to an end. We could understandably have misread John's statement that way, but we would have been wrong. Subsequent events are clear that immersion was not replaced by some kind of "baptism in the Spirit" that did not involve real bodies going into real water. That did not happen in the ministry of Jesus or the ministry of the early church.

What we find is Jesus, in his Great Commission, commanding the baptism of disciples in the name of the Father, the Son and the Spirit. Then Peter soon afterward is heard preaching that repentance and baptism would bring the forgiveness of sins and the gift of the Spirit.

As we look at passages in the New Testament that follow, we find baptism is presented consistently as conversion baptism or transformational baptism. Just look carefully at the context of every baptismal text. It is the place where the old life ends and a new life begins.

But here is the important point in this chapter: This can only happen through the power of the Spirit. As we yield, cry out to God and are immersed, the Spirit washes and regenerates (Titus 3:5).

Are we talking about what some people negatively refer to as "baptismal regeneration"? No, this is a very misleading phrase. We are talking Spirit-powered, Spirit-produced regeneration that happens when one is buried with Christ and is raised up with him to a new life.

In our next chapter we will be looking at the relationship of baptism to life in the Body of Christ. However, since this thought is also related to the Spirit, we should mention a key passage here:

> The body is a unit, though it is made up of many parts; and though all its parts are many, they form one body. So it is with Christ. For we were all baptized by one Spirit into one body—whether Jews or Greeks, slave or free—and we were all given the one Spirit to drink. (1 Corinthians 12:12–13)

There is no reason to think Paul is speaking of baptism in any other way than the time they were immersed in water (see 1 Corinthians 1:13–14). He is not talking about some other inward or mystical experience that was more "spiritual." Since we have already stressed that baptism is much more something that God does than something we do, it should not be surprising to hear that we were baptized (passive voice) *by the one Spirit.*

Baptism is done in physical water, and we are in the hands of another person, just as Jesus was with John, but it is the Spirit that is at work. It is no different from Acts 2 where we see the apostles speaking in other languages with tongues of fire over them; the Spirit was at work in real historical events making it all happen. Paul is speaking to a fractured Corinthian church where so many were trying to get "one up" on each other. He reminds them that the one Spirit who gave each of them their spiritual gifts also was involved in bringing them all into the one body and giving them all himself from which to drink.

## All Comes Together in Baptism

We must try to envision several elements all coming together in a new birth. There is Jesus' death, burial and resurrection—the heart of the gospel. Then, there is our faith produced by the preaching of the Word, our confession of Jesus as Lord, our repentance and rejection of the old life, the death of the old man of sin, our burial with Christ in baptism, and God's gift and our reception of the Spirit who raises us up from the dead to new life and brings us into the Body of Christ. It would not be correct to illustrate the experiences something like this (figure C):

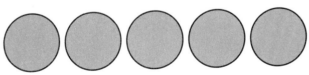

Figure C

No, these are not steps that are in a sequence one after the other, but they are all united, much as we see below (figure D), and overlapping in producing our transformation.

Figure D

For the purposes of this study, we have broken several of these apart in separate chapters, but in reality this cannot be done. It is not even right to say the Spirit has no role until we have shown faith and have repented. The Spirit is at work in the whole process, bringing people together as we see in the book of Acts, and, according to Jesus, it is the Spirit who convicts us of guilt in regard to sin and righteousness and judgment (John 16:8).

Truly, we are "converted" and baptized by the one Spirit. It is the work of the Spirit of God from beginning to end bringing all these themes and events together as one.

### Romans Is Foundational

We have seen that Romans 6 is a very foundational passage for the theme of this book, but we actually should think of the whole book of Romans as being foundational. What Paul says in Romans 4 has a relationship to what he says in Romans 6, and in the same way what he says in Romans 6 is related to what comes a few verses later in Romans 8 (no intention to slight chapters 5 and 7 which are also vital). But let us look at the flow from Romans 6 into Romans 8 as we consider baptism and the Spirit.

We have looked at chapter 6 from several different angles, but basically we have understood Paul to say, "How can we go on in sin since we have been united with Christ in his death and burial in baptism and raised out of this to live a new life?" This idea was followed with a number of statements about no longer letting ourselves be slaves of sin, but instead being slaves of righteousness.

It is interesting that in chapter 6 Paul makes no reference to the Spirit, but is that because the Spirit was not related to what he was saying? I would rather suggest that Paul was facing the same challenge I do in writing this book. There were many overlapping ideas, but he could not talk about everything at the same time. Remember there were no chapters in Paul's original work, but we can still say he makes up for lost ground in chapter 8, in which he mentions the Spirit fourteen times. We must make the greatest connection between these two chapters. Look at the theme passages of the two chapters, which are all a part of the flow of Paul's thought:

> We were therefore buried with him through bap-
> tism into death in order that, just as Christ was
> raised from the dead through the glory of the Fa-
> ther, we too may live a new life. (Romans 6:4)

> And if the Spirit of him who raised Jesus from the
> dead is living in you, he who raised Christ from the
> dead will also give life to your mortal bodies through
> his Spirit, who lives in you. (Romans 8:11)

When Jesus came forth from the tomb, his same body came forth. Or did it? In one sense it was the same. He could be recognized. The marks were in his hands and his side. But in another sense he represented a whole new order of life, apparently as it will be for all of us in the age to come (e.g., he could appear in a room behind locked doors).

Similarly, when we emerge from baptism and give someone a wet hug, we look the same, only a bit odd, standing there dripping. But we are not the same. The very Spirit that raised Jesus from the dead now lives in us and gives life (spiritual life) to our mortal bodies. The Kingdom has come to us. We now belong to the age to come.

The Holy Spirit, who was working to reach us but was not in us, is now in us. And this is the key to everything that has happened and will happen. *We have been born of the Spirit.* The Spirit who is not mentioned in chapter 6 is really responsible for everything that is said there, as chapter 8 makes clear.

With this paradigm we will examine Romans 6 and 8 in a way you have probably never read them before. Instead of looking at these texts as separate ideas, I want to show what they look like when we merge them and realize that this is what it looks like when we superimpose the regenerating work of the Spirit on to our union with Christ in baptism.

---

Romans 6:6: For we know that our old self was crucified with him so that the body of sin might be done away with, that we should no longer be slaves to sin—

> Romans 8:4: ...in order that the righteous requirements of the law might be fully met in us, who do not live according to the sinful nature but according to the Spirit.

---

Our old self was crucified with him, but once we give the sinful nature over to death, something must replace it.

If all that happens in baptism is that we die to sin, we will be like the house Jesus described in Matthew 12. The evil spirit is swept out but then returns to find nothing has replaced it. He promptly invites seven of his friends and moves back in, making the situation even worse than it was before. But in our case, the Spirit does more than work on us, he moves in and is available 24/7 so we do not depend anymore on the old sinful nature but on a new Counselor.

> Romans 6:7–8: …because anyone who has died has been freed from sin. Now if we died with Christ, we believe that we will also live with him.
>
> Romans 8:6: The mind of sinful man is death, but the mind controlled by the Spirit is life and peace…

The reason we needed to die and let the old self be buried is that he or she was fixated on self and filled with the desire to be in control but finding this is never fully possible. No matter how much power or control we gain, it is never enough. But when we trust that the Spirit of God is moving on the face of our waters, we can take a deep breath, enjoy life and feel God's peace. This, too, is living the baptized life.

> Romans 6:11–12: In the same way, count yourselves dead to sin but alive to God in Christ Jesus. Therefore do not let sin reign in your mortal body so that you obey its evil desires.
>
> Romans 8:9: You, however, are controlled not by the sinful nature but by the Spirit, if the Spirit of God lives in you. And if anyone does not have the Spirit of Christ, he does not belong to Christ

Maybe you have heard that Google is designing a car that drives itself. I remember reading years ago that we might eventually get to such a point. It seemed impossible to me, but that was before I had ever heard of GPS. Now it seems quite possible. But in our new post-baptism lives we will never be on automatic pilot or even cruise control.

We have to consciously and deliberately continue to live our baptism—that is really what this book is all about. Sin will continue to present itself, and we must continue to count ourselves dead to it and refuse to obey its evil desire. But we rise out of baptism indwelt by the Spirit of God—the Holy Spirit—the Spirit of Christ. We were baptized in the name of the Father, the Son and the Holy Spirit, and now we have the Spirit because we belong to the Father, the Son and Holy Spirit.

There will still be times of confusion. There will still

be times when we wrestle with the world, but we are no longer controlled by the world or our sinful nature. We are controlled by the Spirit. And we can choose to yield again and again to the Spirit.

It is said that when the spiritual battles became intense in his life, Martin Luther would pound his desk and say, "I am baptized! I am baptized!" That is a good thing to say, particularly as we keep in mind that it is all about the power of the Spirit.

> Romans 6:17: But thanks be to God that, though you used to be slaves to sin, you wholeheartedly obeyed the form of teaching to which you were entrusted.
>
> ---
>
> Romans 8:15–16: For you did not receive a spirit that makes you a slave again to fear, but you received the Spirit of sonship. And by him we cry, "Abba, Father." The Spirit himself testifies with our spirit that we are God's children.

At one time we were trapped by sin, knee deep in it and enslaved to it. Then the good news of deliverance was taught to us, and we yielded and gave our whole hearts to God in Christ. This then brought the Spirit that brings the opposite of fear and bondage. When one dies to self, one really does find his life, because he receives the Spirit of sonship or daughterhood, if you will.

That means we now know God. We know God as *Abba*, Father. You can't get more personal or close than this. We have his ear. We are the apple of his eye. It is like going from the jailhouse to the throne room where we are a child of the King. Remember chapter 2 on grace. The Spirit has raised us up, and in living the baptized life we can feel secure and confident in our identity.

Romans 6:19: I put this in human terms because you are weak in your natural selves. Just as you used to offer the parts of your body in slavery to impurity and to ever-increasing wickedness, so now offer them in slavery to righteousness leading to holiness.

Romans 8:26: In the same way, the Spirit helps us in our weakness. We do not know what we ought to pray for, but the Spirit himself intercedes for us with groans that words cannot express.

Even a clear identity does not take away our weakness. We are the children of the King in his Kingdom, but for now we are still in the present age. The power of the age to come is already at work in us, but our humanity means there is still a struggle. However, the Spirit does not scold us or ridicule us in our weakness. He does not say, "What kind of Christian are you; don't you know how to pray?" No, true to the name Jesus gave him in John 14–16, he *helps* us in our weakness and intercedes for us even when we fail in the most fundamental of spiritual exercises, and that is prayer.

---

Romans 6:22–23: But now that you have been set free from sin and have become slaves to God, the benefit you reap leads to holiness, and the result is eternal life. For the wages of sin is death, but the gift of God is eternal life in Christ Jesus our Lord.

Romans 8:23–24: Not only so, but we ourselves, who have the firstfruits of the Spirit, groan inwardly as we wait eagerly for our adoption as sons, the redemption of our bodies. For in this hope we were saved. But hope that is seen is no hope at all. Who hopes for what he already has?

---

Though they describe the new life from two different angles, chapters 6 and 8 show people fueled by a common hope produced by one Spirit. The baptized life, which is the same as the new life empowered by the Spirit, leads to benefits and fruits that give evidence of even greater things to come.

The baptized life is life in the Spirit. It is a life that affirms the Spirit as the source of our new life, and shows faith that he continues to be at work in us individually and collectively in the body of Christ.

*But we, little fishes after the example of our Ichthus (ΙΧΘΥΣ), Jesus Christ, are born in water, nor have we safety in any other way than by permanently abiding in water…*

## Questions for
## Study and Discussion

1. John the Baptizer said, "I baptize you with water for repentance. But after me will come one who is more powerful than I, whose sandals I am not fit to carry. He will baptize you with the Holy Spirit and with fire" (Matthew 3:11). This might seem to indicate water baptism would be replaced. How do we know such an understanding would be wrong?

2. How does the connection between the Holy Spirit and baptism underscore the idea that baptism in the New Testament is conversion baptism?

3. When you think of your baptism, what thoughts do you have about the Holy Spirit? Reflect on and comment on your answer.

4. Think of some of the things we have seen about living the baptized life. Why is the Holy Spirit so important in the living of this life?

5. What can you do to become more conscious of the work of the Spirit?

# 8

# BAPTISM
# AND
# CHRIST'S BODY

Try for a moment to imagine being part of the crowd during the Pentecost Festival some fifty days after Jesus had been crucified. You do not live in Jerusalem, but you have come there for this special occasion from your own home in Cappadocia (the central part of what is today known as Turkey).

You mingle among the crowd composed of local residents and members of the Jewish diaspora, like yourself, from dozens of cities or regions of the world.

Suddenly you hear several languages being spoken at once. Amidst the din you pick out someone speaking in the language of the Cappadocians, and you hear him clearly, but then in the cacophony it eventually becomes evident that everyone is hearing in their own language. You stand in amazement at the miracle that is taking place around you.

Questions are shouted to the speakers. One of them emerges as the chief spokesman. He addresses the crowd about how a man named Jesus of Nazareth has fulfilled Old Testament prophecy by coming as Israel's Messiah. He speaks of this Jesus' death and his resurrection. His message combined with the miraculous events of the day is powerful and compelling. Your heart is pierced. You are among several who shout, "Brothers, what shall we do?" You will never forget his answer: "Repent and be immersed, every one of you, in the name of Jesus Christ for the forgiveness of your sins. And you will receive the gift of the Holy Spirit."

You and hundreds of others are eager to respond. You queue up at one of the many pools of water in the temple area. Everywhere you look people are being immersed in the name of Jesus. The scene is surreal. When you spent months planning your trip, this was the last thing you expected would happen. You have no idea what all this will mean for your future, but you do know you are committing yourself to this Jesus as both Lord and Messiah.

Decades later, after growing in your understanding and faith and after enduring many trials for your convictions back in Cappadocia, you are now well along in years.

One day a manuscript is brought to your city by a fellow believer, and the elders in your congregation make plans to read it to the disciples. It is an anonymous work, but the messenger says that it was penned by Luke, who traveled with Paul in these very parts. You listen with some amazement as it begins by describing those events in Jerusalem that you were a part of so long ago.

Peter's sermon is recounted, the numerous baptisms are described, and then you hear these statements that bring back a flood of memories:

> They devoted themselves to the apostles' teaching and to the fellowship, to the breaking of bread and to prayer. Everyone was filled with awe, and many wonders and miraculous signs were done by the apostles. All the believers were together and had everything in common.... All the believers were one in heart and mind. No one claimed that any of his possessions was his own, but they shared everything they had.

While you didn't totally understand it that first day, your decision to follow Jesus and be baptized in his name meant you were also being brought into a fellowship that would carry on his work and would even be called his body. As you and others devoted yourselves to the teaching of the apostles, they soon taught you that you were part of the new messianic community that would be living out the attitudes and principles of the Kingdom of God.

Though you were almost literally still wet behind the ears, you and the others learned quickly that commitment to Jesus was no solitary affair. All around you were radical expressions of people sharing their lives together.

### Baptism Places Us in the Body of Christ

This fictional, though plausible, account captures an aspect of baptism that we have only made some passing allusions to so far. However, no picture of the baptized life would be complete without clearly understanding that baptism not only brings us into a relationship with Christ, but places us in the body of Christ and brings us into a new order of relationships with others. Beasley-Murray describes it this way:

> The really important fact, then, of which we have to take account is the indivisibility of the two aspects of baptism: it is baptism to Christ and into the Body. It is at once intensely personal and completely corporate, involving the believer in relationship simultaneously with the Head and with all the members of the Body.[1]

So much in our culture is focused on the individual, and often spiritual experiences are shaped by the perspective of individualism. More and more people are now describing themselves as being spiritual but not being

---

1. Beasley-Murray, *Baptism*, 282.

religious, which is usually another way of saying, "I just like doing my own thing without being connected to something organized or to some group."

However, as we see in the account of Acts 2 that we only partially fictionalized above, baptism did have the two aspects that Beasley-Murray refers to.

First of all it brought one to union with Christ, which is, as we have stressed, that which gives baptism all its meaning. But because Jesus was calling together a community that would live his kingdom message and herald it to the world, baptism also brought one into that community.

Beyond the example in Acts, we have Paul giving some clear teaching on this in several places. Again, to the divided church in Corinth with tendencies much like those we find in the Western world today, he wrote these words that we looked at in the previous chapter:

> The body is a unit, though it is made up of many parts; and though all its parts are many, they form one body. So it is with Christ. For we were all baptized by one Spirit into one body—whether Jews or Greeks, slave or free—and we were all given the one Spirit to drink. (1 Corinthians 12:12–13)

We looked at this passage earlier to emphasize the agency of the Spirit, but Paul's main intention was to help them see that the same Spirit had brought all of them into one body. In that context, their petty arguments about who had the greatest gifts and their failure to work together in unity not only made no sense, it was destroying the work of God. Paul's baptismal language is clear: In baptism we are immersed into one body by the one Spirit. Since we described in the last chapter how it is the Spirit who baptizes us even when we are immersed in water by another person, we don't need to cover that ground again. Here we just need to emphasize that there is no separating baptism into Christ and baptism into his body—the church. Living the baptized life, then, is more than living a spiritual life and a moral life; it is a *connected* life—a shared life. The Greek word for fellowship used in Acts 2 is *kononia,* and it means "sharing together in a common life." In baptism we plunge into this life lived with others and for others.

## *All One in Christ Jesus*

You will notice in 2 Corinthians 12 that Paul specifically mentions various racial, ethnic or societal groups from which the Christians have come, and he's clearly saying that those distinctions now come to an end as a result of baptism into Christ. People in the group relate to one another based on their common relationship with Christ. All other labels and distinctions are part of the old life and have no part in the Kingdom of God. This understanding is developed even further in Galatians 3:

> You are all sons of God through faith in Christ Jesus,
> for all of you who were baptized into Christ have
> clothed yourselves with Christ. There is neither Jew
> nor Greek, slave nor free, male nor female, for you
> are all one in Christ Jesus. If you belong to Christ,
> then you are Abraham's seed, and heirs according to
> the promise. (vv26–29)

In being baptized with faith in Christ, Paul says they have clothed themselves with Christ, and that reality now overrides every other identity they may have. From a spiritual perspective they are neither Jew nor Greek, slave nor free, male nor female, but are all one in Christ Jesus. This is a powerful and far-reaching idea that lets us know just how much has changed in our baptism.

This kind of talk was radical. To say, "neither...male nor female" was especially revolutionary. To make such a statement ran the risk of opening up a whole can of worms, but Paul was willing to go there to highlight the profound transformation of being clothed with Christ in baptism.

We find similar language in Paul's letter to the Colossians. In chapter 3 he writes,

> Do not lie to each other, since you have taken off
> your old self with its practices and have put on the
> new self, which is being renewed in knowledge in
> the image of its Creator. Here there is no Greek or

Jew, circumcised or uncircumcised, barbarian,
Scythian, slave or free, but Christ is all, and is in all.
(vv9–11)

Again, we are told of the end of all the old categories
and divisions. He doesn't mention baptism here, but with
his reference to the old self and the new self, he is still
building on what he said earlier in chapter 2:

In him you were also circumcised, in the putting off
of the sinful nature, not with a circumcision done by
the hands of men but with the circumcision done by
Christ, having been buried with him in baptism and
raised with him through your faith in the power of
God, who raised him from the dead. (vv11–12)

So we see that in all three cases where Paul describes a
new way of thinking about ethnic and social and even gender categories for those in the church, there is a connection
made to baptism, which is seen as a place of radical
change.

This is yet another discussion demonstrating that the
historical tendency to marginalize baptism and make it
simply a symbolic act or an item on a checklist of good
deeds undermines a profound New Testament theme. For
Paul to bring up baptism in these contexts shows just what
a transformational moment it was seen to be. We can

hardly see him basing a crucial appeal to end major divisions or prejudices by appealing to their baptism unless it is central and rich in meaning.

### Practical Implications of Being in the Body

What are the implications for those living the baptized life? First, it is to immerse yourself in the fellowship—that shared common life. It is no longer to see yourself as an individual who is just protecting what is yours and advancing your agenda, but rather to see yourself as one part among many valuable parts that are all being brought together by God's Spirit to live his will on earth as it is heaven.

Second, it is to appreciate that you have been brought together with others because they need you and you need them. We all need each other in order to become all God intends us to be. Others will help you and you will help them. Such a plan is entirely consistent with dying to the old self, which is dominated by a prideful, arrogant, self-interested heart. It fits with putting on the new self which looks after the interest of others.

Third, it is to see that in baptism our old national, ethnic, racial, social and gender classifications died and so did those of others who have been baptized into Christ. Now we are a new humanity. This doesn't mean we renounce our race or nationality or that we don't recognize and respect the heritage of those different from us. It doesn't mean that we, in silly or foolish ways, ignore the differences in men and women. But it does mean that value and worth within the fellowship are never assigned on the basis of those categories and labels.

It means privileges are never given or withdrawn on the basis of such things. It means love is never withheld from some or given to others on the basis of those terms. It is always more comfortable to be with those who are like us, but those who are serious about being the body of Christ recognize how important it is to overcome the discomfort and be a witness to the world of how different things are in the Kingdom.

In some traditions, baptism is primarily about church membership. Often people see it as something they do to join the church. Biblically, baptism is first of all about Jesus Christ, and then because of Jesus' relationship to the church, baptism is about the church. To unite with Christ is to love what he loved, and he loved the church and "gave himself up for her" (Ephesians 5:25).

Living the baptized life will always mean sharing together in the common life of God's people—accepting, forgiving, encouraging, strengthening, challenging and comforting. It will mean loving the church as Jesus loves it.[2]

---

2. For much more on this aspect of the baptized life, see *One Another: God's Plan for Transformational Relationships in the Body of Christ*, cowritten by this author and Steve Brown (www.dpibooks.org).

## Brothers and Sisters in Christ

As I was writing this chapter, I had a surprising conversation with Bob, a brother in our congregation, which caused the two of us to suspect that we might be related. As we checked out some family records, quite quickly our suspicion was confirmed, and then we spent several days researching some of the details, and discussing common ancestors and places our respective families had lived.

I soon talked with Bob's brother, Bill, who lives several hours away. He had been investigating family connections for thirty years, and had, to my amazement, actually interviewed my grandmother at the beginning of his research, never making any connection between her and me.

I had heard about people who became excited about genealogies and family history, but quite unexpectedly, I found it happening to me. Suddenly the burg of Waterloo, Alabama, (population 250)—a place where I spent many days in my childhood learning about fishing, hog killing and gardening from my grandfather—was often in our conversation.

But more significantly, Bob, Bill and I, who are all brothers in Christ, and who have known each other for some time, found ourselves feeling a special kinship and being more eager to be in touch. After all, we are kin!

All of this has been quite fun, but I also know that the

Spirit wants to work in such times to teach us a deeper understanding of God's will. As I have reflected on my experience, it has made me more deeply appreciate all my brothers and sisters in Christ. Now I look around me in the fellowship at my spiritual family. As exciting as my little discovery has been, I realize that I share with each of them something more important than a family name or an obscure small town.

In baptism I have been clothed with Christ and so have they. I have been adopted by the Father and given his very Spirit, but so have they. And we are not just third cousins once removed. We are brothers and sisters in the only family that will really last. Living the baptized life means showing the world that we are one in Christ. It means sharing the good news of the Kingdom with all nations, with all ethnic groups, and letting them know that they, also, can be a part of God's big family.

*For this reason let everyone esteem his Baptism as a daily dress in which he is to walk constantly....*

# Questions for
# Study and Discussion

1. Look back at the quote from Martin Luther found in chapter 1 on page 24. What thoughts do you have about his comment at this point in our study? Are your thoughts any different now from what you felt at first?

2. The Spirit is said to baptize us into one body. What are the implications of the Spirit being connected to the one body?

3. What is so dangerous and so unbiblical about approaching the idea of salvation or a relationship with God with a spirit of individualism?

4. If living the baptized life means giving up all the ways we put people in categories and boxes, what is the greatest challenge for you?

5. We all tend to be drawn to those who are like us. Why do you think it is important for those of us in Christ to make special efforts to develop close relationships with those who are not like us but are also in Christ?

6. What are the greatest blessings of living the baptized life within the body of Christ, the fellowship of believers?

# **9**

# **BAPTISM AND FAITH**

"Woe to you, teachers of the law and Pharisees, you hypocrites! You give a tenth of your spices—mint, dill and cummin. But you have neglected the more important matters of the law—justice, mercy and faithfulness. You should have practiced the latter, without neglecting the former."

Matthew 23:23

Most of us reading this book have been in literally hundreds and probably thousands of classes where we sat and listened to someone teach. While we are able to read, write and understand many concepts including spiritual ones as a cumulative result of those classes, the truth is we remember very few of those individual classes in any detail. If I were asked what classes I remember most clearly, one immediately comes to my mind. I was in my late twenties.

The teacher was an older brother in the faith who was spending a few days with our congregation. He taught a class on Sunday morning based on this passage from Matthew 23, and the way he taught it engraved it on my heart forever.

"How did the Pharisees view the will of God? How did Jesus view the will of God? What was the difference?" the teacher rhetorically asked the class. He drew on the blackboard four or five rectangles standing upright. "The Pharisees," he said, "viewed the will of God much as you would view a set of dominoes or a set of blocks, with each block having the same weight and the same size."

Then he drew a circular archery target with a bull's-eye in the middle. "Jesus, on the other hand, viewed God's will more like this (pointing at the bull's-eye) with certain things more central and more important than others." The teacher quoted from the King James Version, where Jesus says, "You neglected the weightier matters of the law."

He went on to teach that everything in God's will is valuable and significant, but there are some areas that are more crucial and more central. Other things depend on having those most crucial things in place first. This was not a new idea for me. It did not represent a major paradigm shift. But his simple illustration, contrasting the blocks with the target, gave me a tool that I would use countless times the rest of my life. What Jesus taught here is vital in biblical interpretation or hermeneutics. It is vital for living the spiritual life.

### Center of the Target

We always need to be concerned about what is at the center of the target, and for obvious reasons, we would have to put God's love and his grace at the very center. However, as far as the human side is concerned, nothing is more crucial than faith. Overwhelmingly, it is the dominant word used in Scripture to describe the needed response to the gospel. In *Strong in the Grace* I wrote these words:

> There are 472 occurrences of the word "faith" or a form of the words "trust" or "believe" in the New Testament. This is an astounding number. Compare that to 200 references to "love," approximately 100 references to some form of the word "baptize," 75 references to "hope," 68 references to some form of the word "obey," and 52 references to some form of the word "repent." Of course, it is only by examining some of the key texts that we see the significance of faith, but the sheer number of references shows us this was the primary element in the response to the good news.[1]

I then listed the full text of thirty-six passages that

---

1. Thomas A. Jones, *Strong in the Grace* (Spring Hill, TN: DPI, 2004), 47–48.

showed that the primary God-ordained response to the grace that comes through Christ is faith. Here is but a sample of those texts:

## John 6:28–29

> Then they asked him, "What must we do to do the works God requires?"
>
> Jesus answered, "The work of God is this: to believe in the one he has sent."

## Acts 20:21

> I have declared to both Jews and Greeks that they must turn to God in repentance and have faith in our Lord Jesus.

## Romans 1:17

> For in the gospel a righteousness from God is revealed, a righteousness that is by faith from first to last, just as it is written: "The righteous will live by faith."

## Romans 5:1–2

> Therefore, since we have been justified through faith, we have peace with God through our Lord Jesus Christ, through whom we have gained access by faith into this grace in which we now stand. And we rejoice in the hope of the glory of God.

## Galatians 3:11

Clearly no one is justified before God by the law, because, "The righteous will live by faith."

## Ephesians 2:8

For it is by grace you have been saved, through faith—and this not from yourselves, it is the gift of God.

With these and nearly thirty other passages in the New Testament, I showed how a person is justified—that is, put right with God—by faith. The words for "believe" and "faith" in Greek are *pisteo* and *pistis,* respectively, and they mean more than intellectual belief; rather, they have to do with trust. I may believe that the basic facts about Jesus are true, but biblical faith means putting my trust in him, not just having certain ideas about him.

Thus, what enables us to receive the grace of God and what justifies us in his sight is our trust in and our reliance on Jesus, his kingdom message, his death and his resurrection.

Jesus' first recorded words in his ministry were these: "The time is fulfilled, and the kingdom of God is at hand; repent and believe in the gospel" (Mark 1:15 NASB). Repentance is vital, for it means turning away from trusting ourselves, our plans and our performance. It also means turning away from trusting in money, power, pleasure and other false gods of our day. Believing means trusting in the good news of his Kingdom and what Jesus has done.

Some speak of "faith alone," but that is a misleading phrase and one you will not find in Scripture, simply because true faith is never "alone." It is always accompanied by obedience (Romans 1:5). But, this is important: Neither our actions nor our performance brings us to God. We are brought to God by our faith, our trust, in him (Romans 4:5).

In our study we have seen that amazing grace comes to us in baptism. As Luther said, the blessings of baptism are so great that we may doubt they could all be true. But here is what we must understand: Everything said in the New Testament about the effects of baptism can only be said if there is something else present that is even closer to the center of the target, and that is faith.

As atoms are the fundamental building blocks of matter, as amino acids are often said to be the fundamental building blocks of life, faith is the fundamental building block of the spiritual life…and of baptism itself. Baptism is important. We are reminded to recall it and understand what happened there. But faith is more important. It is more fundamental.

So one might honestly ask, "If faith is so vital and something greater than baptism, why is baptism even needed? Why even speak of the baptized life? Why not just write about the faithful life? Why even focus on the lesser, when we have the greater?

In reality, some groups have gone down that road, and as far as one can go. Forty years ago I read several books by a certain author that influenced me greatly. They still sit on my bookshelves today. I had one occasion to go hear him speak. However, I later discovered that he was with one of two well-known denominations that do not practice baptism at all.

While most groups have not gone that far, many have seen faith to be so much more important than baptism that the latter, at best, gets (1) a footnote in their theology and (2) maybe a Sunday or two a year to make sure everybody has "done it." But that hardly fits with the baptismal texts we have examined in this book that are all transformational in nature.

### Bringing Faith and Baptism Together

So how do we bring these two together? On the one hand, we have faith—a fundamental building block and at the very center of the target. On the other hand, we have baptism—spoken of in rich and meaningful terms but clearly the lesser. How do we view their relationship? It is probably not so complicated.

First, we don't want to make little of baptism, since that is certainly not what the Scriptures do.

Second, we don't want to elevate baptism and give it some power or meaning Scripture does not give it, always remembering that it is not as great as faith.

Third, we want to look at the texts that show how faith and baptism are brought together and what relationship they have to each other.

Finally, having heard the Scriptures, we must trust God, letting Scripture guide us and not logic or tradition.

There are two passages that can help us here because they are the only two that speak directly to the interplay of faith and baptism. The first of these is in Galatians 3, which we have noted before in another context:

> You are all sons of God through faith in Christ Jesus, for all of you who were baptized into Christ have clothed yourselves with Christ. There is neither Jew nor Greek, slave nor free, male nor female, for you are all one in Christ Jesus. (vv26–28)

We should again be reminded that the context of this passage is a letter written to advocate for justification by faith and to counter those who want to return to justification that depends upon human effort, performance and keeping of law. It is also written to challenge those who would withhold their fellowship from believers whom they deem to be defective because they don't keep these rules they have added to the gospel.

To this situation Paul makes the most fundamental statement of all: *You are all—that means all of you—children of God through faith, through your trust in Jesus Christ, not through your performance or your human effort.* But then he adds a parallel statement: *For all of you who were baptized into Christ have clothed yourselves with Christ or have put on Christ like a garment.*

We cannot argue that baptism is parallel to faith because it is of equal weight to faith, but in this case, it is parallel because baptism was linked to faith and was an instrument of faith in bringing them all into Christ, where they all now wear the same garment—namely Christ.

As a young minister and teacher, I was privileged (exactly how I don't remember) to attend a special seminar, limited to one hundred participants, led by the famous British Baptist scholar G.R. Beasley-Murray whose famous work—*Baptism in the New Testament*—I have quoted several times. The series was focused on the theme of "Baptism and Christian Unity." When he spoke of this passage, I remember him, holding out his arm, taking the cuff of his shirt and turning it inside out and then back and forth and saying, "Faith and baptism are the inside and the outside of the same thing—our coming to God."

This was an "Ah-ha" moment for me. Baptism is not in some "human effort" category; baptism is in the category of faith. Faith and baptism are the inside and the outside of the same response to God's grace. This is the only reason Paul would bring baptism up, particularly in this context, in the same sentence with this vital concept of faith. In our new birth experience, baptism is seen as faith—as an expression of faith.

The second passage is also one we have looked at earlier with another emphasis. It is found in Colossians 2:

> In him you were also circumcised, in the putting off of the sinful nature, not with a circumcision done by the hands of men but with the circumcision done by Christ, having been buried with him in baptism and raised with him through your faith in the power of God, who raised him from the dead. (vv11–12)

In Galatians 3 faith was spoken of first, then baptism, but with the two clearly united. In this case baptism is spoken of first, but very quickly, another phrase concerning faith is added so that we are reminded of the inward part of the response that gives it its meaning. We are buried with Christ in baptism *and raised with him through our faith*, our trust, in the power of God and in what he did in raising Jesus from the dead.

Our baptism is a crucial event in our personal history. It was there that we put off the sinful nature and were buried with Christ and raised to a new life. But baptism is not a magical ceremony. It is the sign of something far more significant than itself—our faith, our trust and our surrender to the power of God, so one can speak of baptism and faith as united. And so it was through our faith that this event—our baptism—was transformational. Galatians 3 teaches that faith and baptism are the inside and the outside of the same thing. Colossians 2 reverses the order and teaches that baptism and faith are the outside and inside of the same thing. In both cases, what really saves us and transforms us is *the object* of our faith and our baptism. We place our faith in Jesus Christ; we are baptized to Jesus Christ. Faith and baptism are united in their focus on Christ, who is the one who makes us new.

## Do Not Separate the Two

Now having heard what the Scriptures say about the relationship between faith and baptism, we must trust what we have heard and be careful because "what God has joined together let man not separate" (Mark 10:9). Though Jesus made that statement in regard to marriage, it applies to faith and baptism and any matters God has brought together.

Some people, it seems, want to share their lives together as a married couple but say, "Why do we need a ceremony, or what's so important about a piece of paper? Isn't the important issue that we love each other and are committed to each other?" In one sense, they are right. Their love and commitment are more important than the license and the ceremony. I suppose that we could think like that and say, "Why do we need baptism; isn't the important thing our faith?" But what we have just read shows us that God willed to keep our faith united with our baptism, and for our baptism to be a rich experience because of faith in the power of God. If we want to be "married" to Jesus, we express this desire and commitment at the "altar" of baptism. So what does this union of faith and baptism mean for living the baptized life?

First, it reminds us that it would be most appropriate to talk about and study living the faithful life. I would have no problem with someone who would argue that we have a much greater basis for writing on that topic than on this one. In some ways, they would be right. I would say, "God bless their work."

Second, however, these texts remind us to look to our baptism and keep on having the faith—hopefully, the humble childlike faith—that brought us there in the first place. Our baptism is the beginning of a faith journey. The baptized life is one where we keep trusting and keep surrendering.

Third, as we go and make disciples as part of the faithful, baptized life, we do not want to simply baptize people;

we want to baptize people who have faith in the power of God. As we study the Scriptures with others and share our lives with them, we do not want them in any way to put their faith in baptism. We don't even want them to put their faith in faith! We want their baptism to be a supreme moment of putting their faith in Christ and the beginning of a new life of living by faith.

Since faith and baptism are so tightly bound together, as the inside and outside the same transformational experience of dying and rising with Christ, everything that is true of living a life of faith is true of living the baptized life. When we are not weakened in our faith but trust that God has the power to do what he's promised, we are living the baptized life. When we obey God and go even though we do not know where we're going, we are living the baptized life. When we suffer in ways that confuse us and perplex us, but we hold to the fact that nothing can separate us from the love of Christ, we are living the baptized life.

Remembering our baptism should not only cause us to remember the death and resurrection of Jesus, but cause us to remember our young faith in what was done for us and remember that that faith needs to keep growing each day.

To live the baptized life is to place our faith in God's lavish grace, to embrace such a great salvation, and to commit ourselves to live in this age as citizens of a new Kingdom. To remember our baptism is to remember that we have died with Christ and been raised with him to a new manner of life and love that can only be lived in the power of the Holy Spirit. It means to understand by faith that we have been plunged into the sea of a new humanity, so that all those who have been born anew are our brothers and our sisters, with no divisions among us.

*There is no story but God's;*
*no God but the Father, Son and Spirit;*
*and no life but the baptized life.*

## Questions for
## Study and Discussion

1. What are your thoughts about the idea that faith is greater than baptism? Explain why you think as you do.

2. Which is more important—the public wedding vow or the intention in the heart of the bride or groom? What is the relationship here between two things of unequal weight or importance? How does this relate to faith and baptism?

3. In bringing people to a decision to follow Jesus and be baptized into him, what are the implications of this teaching about faith and baptism? Do you have a tendency to emphasize one more than the other?

4. As you think about the baptized life being a life of faith, what challenges does this offer to your life?

# CONCLUSION

Quite amazingly, the study of baptism in the New Testament leads one to see an almost complete mosaic showing the life of a disciple. Hopefully, we can see now why Luther was amazed at how many benefits and blessings are tied to baptism.

While this needs to be said, we must also return to an idea expressed at the beginning of our study and say that baptism on its own is nothing at all. God has chosen to use it to bring us into Christ. He uses it to dramatically illustrate the transformation that is affected as we unite with Christ. He uses it to call us to continually remember to be dying and rising with Christ.

Remembering our baptism consistently calls us to live a different life. But on its own, baptism is like a pair of eyeglasses on your bedside table or like a cup sitting in a cabinet. The glasses do you no good unless you put them on and look through the lens and then see your spouse or your child or a beautiful sunset. The cup does you no good if it sits on the shelf and is not filled with a refreshing liquid that will cool you when it's hot and warm you when it's cold. Baptism is nothing unless you see through it your own sinful nature and the realities and grace of the new life in Jesus. It has no value unless it is filled with a living faith that focuses on the power of God that raised Jesus from the dead and can live in us.

The God who brings the new covenant in Jesus has no interest in ritual for ritual's sake. When he gives what some may call a sign and others may call a sacrament, it is for the purpose of connecting with our hearts and bringing us to a new place morally and spiritually.

In his wisdom, God gave us baptism. Remember it is from heaven not from men. That can only mean he knows we need it. We need a line of demarcation. We need a "before and after" moment. We need a decisive time to look back on and reflect on. We know we do, for he gives us nothing to waste our time or energy. But even these truths are powerful only because they involve us with Jesus and refocus us on him.

Don't allow your baptism to be a piece of ancient history. If it was last month or forty years ago, let it be a place you return to often. Remember the grace that came to you there and stay in that grace and splash it on others around you. Rejoice in the Kingdom you were born into and recommit yourself to the kingdom life. Remember how your sins were washed away, but keep walking in the light, confessing your sins, and allowing the blood of Christ to keep on cleansing you.

Relive the moment. See yourself being laid in the watery grave, dead to the old life and buried with Christ, and then raised up with him to live a new way. Check your heart and see if you have wandered from your conviction about dying to sin. Check your faith and see if you are still confident about the Spirit that was given to you to help you live that new life as a citizen of heaven. Remember that baptism into Christ meant baptism into his body and reaffirm your commitment to belong to all the others who make up that body.

Remember Jesus. Remember the cross, the burial and the empty tomb. Remember your baptism. Live the kingdom life, the baptized life, the resurrected life and the life in the body of Christ. And go make disciples, baptizing them, teaching them to obey.

# Appendix 1

*Baptism in the New Testament:*
*An Exercise in Bible Reading*

In chapter 1, I mentioned that several years ago my friend, fellow teacher and fellow author, Steve Brown, and I taught a series on "Baptism in the New Testament." We based the class on Steve's idea for us to go through the New Testament book by book, asking what we can learn about baptism just from reading our English translations of the Bible, *assuming we had no knowledge of Greek*, trying as best we could to hear it for the first time.

At the end of our study we listed twenty-five conclusions we could describe with confidence from the scriptures we had read. Here are those conclusions as they were arrived at starting with the Gospel of Matthew and reading through the New Testament:

1. Baptism is something that is done to you, but you have to come to it.

2. In the case of John's baptism, it is accompanied by the confessing of sins, in response to a call to radical change needed due to the Lord's coming.

3. It must be preceded by a true repentance (that is visible by what it produces) and by humility.

4. It is for the forgiveness of sins, or to wash away sins.

5. It requires plenty of water, often being done in a river, involving going down into and coming up out of the water.

6. Jesus commands everyone who wants to be his disciple to be baptized.

7. Baptism is to be done in the name of the Father, Son and Holy Spirit or in the name of Jesus.

8. Baptism is accompanied by the gift of the Holy Spirit.

9. In another sense, Jesus also promised to personally baptize with the Holy Spirit after he returned to heaven. Examples of this are only found in Acts 2 and 10.

10. Baptism occurs as soon as a person makes the decision to repent and follow Jesus or accept him as Lord. Therefore baptism is always connected to conversion.

11. Faith and repentance and baptism are together and not widely separated experiences.

12. In baptism we die to sin.

13. In baptism we go *into* Christ.

14. In baptism we are united with his death (we go *into* his death).

15. In baptism we are buried with Christ into his death.

16. We come out of baptism raised to a new life.

17. Faith, grace and baptism all go together, baptism getting its meaning from faith in Christ and grace that comes from Christ.

18. Who does the baptizing is unimportant. We are actually all baptized by the One Spirit.

19. None of us should be concerned about how many people we personally baptize.

20. We are all baptized into the one Body—we all are connected through baptism into Christ with the community of faith.

21. Baptism into Christ breaks down all the gender, ethnic and social barriers.

22. Baptism is one of the core teachings on the same level with the other "ones" mentioned in Ephesians that unite all Christians.

23. In baptism the sinful nature is removed as a circumcision done by Christ.

24. It might be one of the elementary teachings about Christ (or the Messiah), one of the things you learn first (although the unusual plural term "baptisms" in Hebrews 6 may indicate something else).

25. Baptism saves you, not because of what is happening physically but what is happening spiritually as you pledge yourself to God (or appeal to God) and connect with Christ's resurrection.

# Appendix 2

## 'Rebaptism'?

I can imagine that some readers of this book may well think of the different aspects of baptism that we have considered and then think of how relatively little they understood at the time of their own baptism. It would not be surprising for some to wonder if their own experience was valid. Before one comes to that conclusion, I would want to suggest that several points be considered based on my study of the New Testament:

1.  There is no such thing as a perfect understanding of baptism either by one studying the subject or certainly by a new believer being baptized to enter the Kingdom of God. Even a person who is baptized after reading a book like this will not understand everything about the subject that could be understood. No doubt at any point in our lives there are shortcomings in the understanding we all have. The efficacy of baptism is not based on perfect understanding but on Jesus, the object of our faith and baptism.

2.  "There can be no retroactive understanding of baptism" is an erroneous teaching. Most, if not all, of us learn many truths about the meaning of our baptism in the days, months and years that follow baptism. This means that much of our understanding of baptism occurs after the fact as we grow in Christ. Our understanding of the baptized life will hopefully keep expanding.

3.  No one in the New Testament who was baptized in the name of Jesus ever had their baptism questioned by a spiritual leader (even if they were doing poorly). The only occasion when people were questioned about their baptism was when it was revealed that they had only been baptized with John's baptism. They were subsequently baptized *in the name of Jesus* for the first time (Acts 19:1–4).

4.  There may be some valid reasons to consider being baptized even when one has had a previous baptism. These could include but would not be limited to the following:

    (a) When a person was "baptized" (actually sprinkled) as an infant or child and was not at all involved in making a decision to repent or trust Jesus.

    (b) When a person was baptized for some reason other than to respond to Jesus (for example, to satisfy a spouse or other person).

(c) When a person believed the exact opposite from what the Scriptures teach (for example, "This baptism has nothing whatsoever to do with my forgiveness").

(d) When a person cannot come to peace about his or her baptism. We must be careful at this point because someone may need counseling and teaching more than they need to be baptized.

5. If a person was originally immersed because of his faith in Jesus, the decision to be baptized again must lie entirely with the individual and should never be imposed on a person by a teacher or a guide. (Again, remember #3 above.) To illustrate the point, if I am studying the Bible with Martin who previously was immersed because of his own faith in Jesus, I may be concerned because he did not understand X (a certain truth) at the time or did not follow up with certain actions. I ought to raise issues to help him clarify his thinking. However, the decision about what to do or not do is Martin's alone as he stands before Jesus.

6. Most people who were taught certain basics about faith, repentance and baptism just need to recommit themselves to the living of the baptized life.

7.  Whatever decision a person makes, disciples can only work together to reach others and bring them into the fellowship if they are united in teaching that faith, repentance and baptism are all part of conversion to Jesus.

8.  When an individual decides her baptism was valid, but then begins to include New Testament teaching about baptism in her own evangelistic message, she may very well reexamine her original conclusion and decide she should, after all, be baptized.

9.  The New Testament examples of baptism in the book of Acts should help us to understand that what we do in being baptized is not the focus, but rather faith in what Jesus has done for us in his death, burial and resurrection. The relatively small amount of time and teaching prior to baptism in these Acts accounts underscores this point well.

10. Once again, in our self-examination, we must not get too focused on ourselves and must never forget that the power of baptism does not come because we do everything right and have every right thought and correct attitude, but because we are coming in baptism to put our faith in Jesus Christ.